MW01280391

Specialties of the Haus

A Cookbook by Edelweiss Publishing
TCM International, Inc.

Copyright 1999
by
Edelweiss Publishing
TCM International, Inc.
Indianapolis and Vienna

First Edition

First Printing   July 1999   10,000

International Standard Book Number: 0-9672236-0-1

Illustrations by Marge Kincade
Edited by Jo Staib

MANUFACTURED IN THE USA BY

cookbook resources

541 Doubletree Drive
Highland Village TX 75067
(972) 317-0245

Forward

*H*aus Edelweiss equips and encourages dedicated men and women from throughout Eastern Europe to transform their own countries, cultures, and churches for Christ. Many serve amidst poverty. Others must reckon with corruption and political strife. Some endure scorn because of their faith or background.

They take everything we can provide and use it with an economy and wisdom that makes partnership with them pure joy. No complaints. Always grateful for any assistance. Ready to serve others in any way they possibly can as they build for their futures.

It is my fervent prayer that this cookbook will be a way to help them even more.

Dr. Tony Twist, Director
TCM International Institute
Heiligenkreuz, Austria

Thank You

*T*here are always many people behind the scenes who help make a project like this one possible. In this case, we feel it surely must be an international "cast of thousands."

Our heartfelt thanks to all of you who, through your enthusiasm, notes, and prayers, have encouraged and supported us during the two years this book has been in the making.

Very special thanks is due to some. To Tracy Bergin who typed and re-typed every word, and offered much helpful editorial comment. To our eagle-eyed proofreaders Patty Crull, Carolyn Dobbs, and Jinnie Helm. To copy editors Carolyn Dobbs and Suzanne Twist. And to Sheryn Jones of Cookbook Resources for the technical help and guidance that carried us through this whole process with our sanity (mostly) intact.

And finally, to all the cooks who have served at Haus Edelweiss over the years, we salute you. Thank you for the tradition of good food served with love which you helped establish and maintain.

Jo Staib
Marge Kincade

Introduction

Welcome to Haus Edelweiss. Just the mention of that name can evoke a kaleidoscope of warm, wonderful memories for those who have shared in the experience of serving at Haus Edelweiss. The picturesque beauty of the park-like grounds and Bavarian-style buildings tucked against the hillside in the Vienna Woods. The remarkable peace and serenity which seems to envelope the entire campus. It is as if the very presence of God hovers there in benediction. But most memorable of all are the people. The dynamics of eighty to one-hundred people from several countries, all with widely different cultures and backgrounds, working, studying, praying together. For many people, it is a heart-changing, once-in-a-lifetime experience.

Here, in an atmosphere of warm hospitality and rich fellowship, Christians from Central and Eastern Europe come to receive seminary training, which, until a few years ago, was unavailable to them in their own countries because of communist control. At Haus Edelweiss bodies and spirits are nourished and hungry minds are fed. An abundance of love, laughter, caring, and sharing are served up daily along with platters and bowls filled with delicious, nourishing food. It is American food, served at traditional American mealtimes; a cross-cultural experience for our Eastern European friends. But oh, my! How enthusiastically it is received! Requests for recipes come almost daily from both Europeans and Americans. In fact, during the three years I served at Haus Edelweiss as Coordinator of Food Services (read "cook"), there were never fewer than six recipe requests at any conference. (The wife of one of our Romanian students asked for seven! She was a new bride and eager to duplicate the dishes her husband was so thoroughly enjoying.) The obvious response to all of this interest was to prepare a cookbook which would feature recipes for the most requested foods served at Haus Edelweiss.

Thus was the dream of **Specialties of The Haus** conceived. The book I envisioned would reflect the attention to quality, beauty, and detail which are typical of every effort at the Haus. It seemed natural to include an International Section featuring foods from the countries TCM serves. This book, I dreamed, must be brimful of colorful art to capture the essence and charm of Haus Edelweiss and the rich traditions of Eastern and Central Europe. And it must contain stories and anecdotes to capture the reader so that each one would sense and savor a small taste of the whole experience of the Haus. But most importantly, I dreamed that proceeds from the sale of this book would be used to provide scholarships for the rapidly growing number of students entering the Institute for Biblical Studies (IBS) program directed by Dr. Tony Twist at Haus Edelweiss.

This very special blend of history, good food, and delightful artwork has been two years in the making. **Specialties of the Haus** contains nearly 200 recipes for hearty, flavorful, uncomplicated food to delight your family and guests, or please the crowd at your next church supper. Page after page is enhanced by the beautiful original watercolor paintings, pencil sketches, and line art of Marge Kincade, former Haus Edelweiss staff member. I think you will especially enjoy the paintings of dolls in the International Section. Much more than a cookbook, we hope this will be a keepsake you will treasure and enjoy for years to come.

During these last few months as Marge and I have worked to bring **Specialties of the Haus** into its final form, we have been overwhelmed again and again with a sense of awe and wonder and deep humility that God would entrust to us this very special project, designed for the sole purpose of expanding His Kingdom. And we have never lost sight of Who has really been the Foreman of this project. He has opened every door to supply the technical guidance and expertise we needed. We have been the fortunate recipients of this rich blessing and ours has truly been a labor of love. We hope you find it as exciting as we do to be a part of equipping and encouraging these committed Christians.

All proceeds from the sale of **Specialties of the Haus** will be used to fund scholarships for students in Central and Eastern Europe entering TCM's Institute.

Willkommen
In Haus Edelweiss

Table of Contents

History and Backgroumd

*T*he work of TCM in Europe began in 1963 when Gene Dulin, founder and first president, established contact with Christians in Russia and Poland. Access to people in countries behind the iron curtain was severely restricted during those early years, but from its base in Toronto, Canada, TCM found ways to supply food, clothing, and medicine to suffering Christians. In 1964, TCM sent Russian New Testaments to Russian Christians. They soon came to know that TCM CARED and was worthy of their trust.

In 1971 a search was begun to find a suitable site in Europe for a ministry base -- a location in a secure area but near enough to Eastern Europe for reasonable access. How little we knew how much the ministry was to grow and expand over the coming years!

An ideal location was found near the village of Heiligenkreuz, 25 kilometers (15 miles) southwest of Vienna, Austria. It was vacant and overgrown, but the potential of the property was apparent. TCM began negotiations to purchase the property that would become known as "Haus Edelweiss."

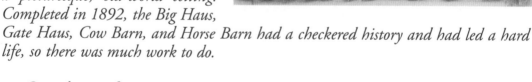

Nestled against the forested hillsides of the Vienna Woods, the Bavarian-style architecture of the four buildings on the site provided a picturesque, old-world setting. Completed in 1892, the Big Haus, Gate Haus, Cow Barn, and Horse Barn had a checkered history and had led a hard life, so there was much work to do.

Over the next five years, extensive renovations were carried out repairing, restoring, and replacing. Offices and apartments soon occupied space which, in the early years of the century, had been home to a stable-full of prized horses. During this same period, the offices of TCM International were moved from Toronto, Canada to Indianapolis, Indiana in the United States.

When communism at last released its iron grip on Eastern Europe and the Berlin Wall fell, TCM was positioned to move ahead with the work for which God had long been preparing. Over the next ten years, dynamic changes took place in Central and Eastern Europe and exciting things began happening at Haus Edelweiss. Now, at last, emerging leaders who had not been allowed to travel, even within their own countries, were able to come to Haus Edelweiss for the training they needed and so desperately wanted.

A schedule of Leadership Training Conferences was drawn up and professors recruited. The hillside behind the Big Haus was carved out to make room for an additional building for leadership training and housing. This new Leadership Training Center (LTC) was dedicated in 1990.

In 1991, TCM's new president, Dr. Tony Twist, established the Institute for Biblical Studies (IBS). A program designed to provide accredited graduate-level instruction, leading to a Master of Arts degree, was now in place. For those not holding a university diploma or unable to complete the M.A. course-work, a Certificate was offered, requiring only half of the credits needed for the M.A. For students desiring help only in specific areas the Simple Audit was offered.

The decade of the 1990s has seen a dizzying array of changes and accomplishments. In the four years since the first class was graduated in 1995, TCM's IBS based at Haus Edelweiss has awarded nine Certificates and forty-four Master of Arts degrees. 110 new students were admitted in 1998. As of early May, 1999 there are 292 students enrolled in the IBS program, including 177 candidates studying for the Master of Arts and another 43 studying for the Master of Divinity degrees. Plans to offer a Ph.D. degree and secure more property in Austria are in process.

Because of the rapid growth of the Institute, all proceeds from this cookbook will be used for student scholarships. Without scholarships the students cannot afford to study. These scholarships come through gifts from individuals, churches, estates, trusts, or other means, such as cookbook sales.

Extension Training Centres have been established in Belarus, Bulgaria, Czech Republic, Estonia, Hungary, Poland, Romania, Russia, and Ukraine. An addition to the Horse Barn, completed in 1994, houses the Graduate Student Center (GSC) with lodging for eighteen resident students, kitchen, and lounge. The IBS library, computer lab, and a small classroom complete the upper level. Below are a large workshop and storage room. In 1997, property adjacent to Haus Edelweiss was purchased and renovated for additional staff and student housing.

During all this growth and change, TCM has continued to supply food, clothing, and medicine to meet urgent needs. Thousands of Bibles and New Testaments, printed in the languages of Central and Eastern Europe, have been distributed as well as children's literature and a variety of inspirational literature. Youth camps have been constructed, assistance provided to plant new churches in Eastern Europe, and help and encouragement supplied in numerous ways.

More exciting changes lie ahead. During 1999-2000, an addition on the east side of the Big Haus will be constructed to expand kitchen space, enlarge the walk-in cooler, and provide a fourth classroom. The upper level, looking out over the hillside, will have much-needed additional housing for visiting professors.

The leaders of TCM International are dedicated to offering nothing less than the best in quality leadership development training to all IBS students. Strong emphasis is placed on basic Biblical values, growing leaders who recognize the importance of character as well as scholarship; servanthood as well as skills.

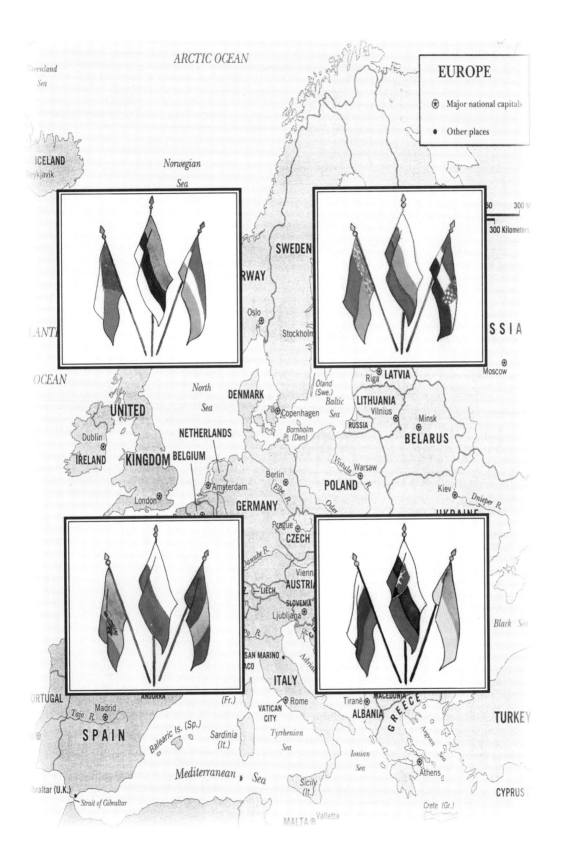

"Dear Everybody at Haus Edelweiss,

We should like to express our thanks for your loving care during this week. Thank you for the teaching. We go back with refreshed energy to serve to the Lord in our families, in our church and everywhere. We love you all and pray for your precious work and for you all personally. God bless you."

Bulgarian Youth Conference

Soups
Sandwiches
Breads

Soup du Jour

Throughout Central and Eastern Europe, soup is a mainstay. It is eaten almost every day, usually at the evening meal, along with bread and perhaps some cheese. Typically the soups are much thinner than those we serve in America—a flavorful broth with small bits of vegetables, perhaps a few thin noodles and (if they are fortunate) a small amount of meat.

At Haus Edelweiss, soup is served two or three times a week, always at lunch, and is a much more substantial meal. For Soup du Jour, we just "make it up" as we go along.

The nicest thing that can happen to leftovers is to be born again in soup. You don't need a recipe, just use what you have and enhance the flavor with your favorite herbs and seasonings.

Start with a good rich broth, either homemade or canned, or made with water and instant chicken bouillon granules. For a family of six, for example, begin with about 8 cups of liquid. Heat the broth in a large kettle. Allow to simmer a few minutes then taste for seasonings (salt, pepper, more bouillon granules?). Meanwhile, cut up any left-over cooked meat you may have (chicken, turkey, pork) and leftover vegetables and stir into broth. Not enough? Add to the broth a few frozen vegetables, perhaps 1/2 cup each corn, green beans, and peas. Let the soup come to the boiling point; reduce heat and simmer for 20 to 30 minutes. Taste again and adjust seasonings. Add a small amount of your favorite herbs—perhaps some parsley and a bit of basil. Dried celery leaves, crumbled, add great flavor. Keep the heat on low and let the soup just simmer a while to blend the flavors.

Shortly before serving, you may decide to add a few fine noodles. Or left-over cooked rice works very well. Left-over gravy from a roast is a great flavor-enhancer for soup; add it to the broth before adding vegetables and meat. Experiment. You may develop your family's next favorite recipe!

Easy Minestrone Soup

6 ounces ground fresh turkey (or ground beef)

3 1/2 cups (2 cans 14 ounces each) beef broth

2 cups (1 can 15 ounces) tomatoes, cut up

2 teaspoons instant beef bouillon

1/2 teaspoon basil

1/2 teaspoon oregano

1/16 teaspoon garlic powder

1 package (10 ounce) frozen mixed vegetables

1 can (15 ounce) navy beans, drained and rinsed

Spray a pan with non-stick vegetable spray. Over medium heat, cook the meat until all pink color is gone, breaking it up as it cooks. Add all the remaining ingredients EXCEPT the beans. Bring to a boil; reduce heat, cover and simmer 1 hour. Add the beans; heat thoroughly. Serves 8.

Cook's Note: A delicious, nutritious soup chock full of vegetables and very low fat, especially when made with ground turkey. This is a dense soup; if you prefer more liquid just add a little more broth. Especially good served with hot corn bread or crusty herb bread.

Italian Vegetable Soup

1 pound ground beef

3/4 cup onion, diced

1/4 teaspoon garlic powder

*4 medium carrots, peeled and
    sliced*

7 cups water

*3 1/2 cups (29 ounce can)
    tomatoes, with juice, cut up*

6 teaspoons instant beef bouillon

1 teaspoon Italian seasoning

1/4 teaspoon pepper

salt to taste

1 1/2 cups small zucchini, sliced

*2 cups (15 or 16 ounce can)
    kidney beans, drained and
    rinsed*

*1 cup uncooked Rotini (corkscrew
    macaroni)*

In a large, heavy pan, brown meat, onion, and garlic powder, breaking up meat as it cooks. Drain off excess fat. Add carrots, water, cut-up tomatoes, instant bouillon, and seasonings. Bring to a boil. Cover, lower heat and simmer about 30 minutes. Taste for salt. Add zucchini, beans, and Rotini. Continue cooking 15 to 20 minutes until Rotini is tender. Serve with Parmesan cheese if desired. Serves 8 to 10.

Cook's Note: A dense, hearty soup, this is almost a meal in itself, and very tasty.

Lentil Soup

2 cups lentils, rinsed

7 cups water

1/2 cup onion, sliced thin

1/8 teaspoon garlic powder

3 stalks celery, sliced

2 medium carrots, sliced thin

3 medium potatoes, peeled and
  diced

1/4 teaspoon pepper

1/2 teaspoon dried basil

salt to taste

2 cups canned tomatoes with
  juice, cut up

1 Tablespoon vinegar

In a large kettle, combine all ingredients EXCEPT tomatoes and vinegar. Bring to a boil; lower heat and simmer 1 1/2 to 2 hours. During the last 1/2 hour, add tomatoes and vinegar. Taste for seasonings. Serves 10 to 12.

Cook's Note: An old-fashioned soup, added to the Haus file by a former cook, and enjoyed especially by our European guests.

Peasant Bean Soup

1 1/4 cups dry pinto beans
1 1/4 cups dry red kidney beans
3/4 cup dry small white beans
1/2 cup lentils
2 small carrots, sliced thin
1/2 cup onion, diced
1/2 cup celery, sliced thin
2 cups canned tomatoes, with
    juice, cut up
1/2 teaspoon garlic powder
1/4 teaspoon pepper
1/2 pound smoked ham,
    diced small
salt to taste

Wash pinto, kidney, and white beans. Rinse lentils and set aside. Place beans in a large pot; add cold water to cover well. Cover pan; soak overnight.

Drain beans; return to pot. Cover with fresh water. Bring to a boil, lower heat and simmer 1 hour. Add lentils, carrots, onion, and celery; continue cooking until beans are tender, adding more water as needed. Add tomatoes, seasonings, and ham. Continue to simmer another 1/2 hour. Serves about 10.

Cook's Note: When cooking dried beans, take care not to add salt (or salty meat) until beans are tender, as salt retards the process and you may end up with beans which simply refuse to cook to a nice, tender texture.

Potato Soup

8 to 10 medium potatoes
    (about 3 pounds)
water to just cover
    (about 4 to 4 1/2 cups)
1/2 teaspoon salt
1/3 to 1/2 cup onion, diced fine
6 Tablespoons margarine
6 Tablespoons flour
6 cups milk
liquid drained from
    cooked potatoes
1/2 teaspoon celery flakes
1/2 teaspoon pepper
1 1/2 teaspoons salt (or to taste)

Peel potatoes and dice small (1/2 inch pieces). Just cover with cold water, add salt; cook until potatoes are tender. Drain, SAVING LIQUID.

Make a thin white sauce: melt margarine, stir in flour, mixing until smooth. Add milk, stirring with a whisk to blend. Bring just to a boil, lower heat and simmer 1 to 2 minutes. Stir in the cooking liquid from the potatoes and all the seasonings. Taste for salt. Add cooked potatoes; stir to blend. Heat thoroughly but do not boil. Makes 3 1/2 quarts.

Cook's Note: If desired, add 1 cup very thin slices of frankfurter to soup—my family's favorite version of Potato Soup.

If you are using diced, left-over cooked potatoes, you need about 8 to 10 cups of diced potatoes. Since there will be no cooking liquid, substitute chicken broth. The onion can be sautéed in the margarine before adding flour to make the white sauce.

Baked Ham 'n Cheese Sandwiches

8 hamburger buns, split
1 pound ham (boiled or baked),
    sliced very thin
1 pound Swiss cheese, sliced thin
1/2 cup margarine, softened
1/4 cup prepared mustard
1/4 cup onion, minced fine
1 Tablespoon poppy seeds
    (optional)

Mix together margarine, mustard, onion, and poppy seeds (if used), blending well.

Spread both cut sides of buns with the butter mixture, using about 1 Tablespoon on each bun half. Place a slice of cheese on EACH half; divide the ham between the sandwiches. Wrap each sandwich in foil. Place on a baking sheet and bake at 350° F for about 15 minutes, until piping hot. Serves 8.

Cook's Note: These are perfect for a do-ahead meal. Easy to prepare, refrigerate, and bake when ready. They can also be prepared ahead and frozen for up to a week or two. Thaw completely before baking. Increase baking time if necessary.

Haus Hint: For large quantities, you can avoid wrapping the sandwiches individually. Arrange them on parchment paper-lined baking sheets, then cover the entire baking sheet with heavy duty foil, sealing the edges well. Increase baking time to 20 minutes. We make 100 to 120 for a lunch at Haus Edelweiss and find this works well.

Oven Grilled Cheese Sandwiches

softened margarine
12 slices sandwich bread
12 slices American
    (or other square cut) cheese

Spread softened margarine on half of bread slices. Place slices, buttered side down, on baking sheet; lay 2 slices of cheese on each. Top with the rest of the bread slices. Spread margarine on tops of slices.

Bake uncovered at 350° F for about 15 to 20 minutes, turning sandwiches over halfway through baking time. Bread should be golden brown and the cheese melty. Do not over-bake. Makes 6 sandwiches.

Cook's Note: At the Haus we fill the ovens with these popular, crusty sandwiches, baking 110 to 120 at a time.

Tuna Melts

Tuna Salad (your favorite recipe
    to serve 4 to 6)
4 to 6 slices sandwich bread
1/2 cup shredded cheese

Spread bread slices generously with tuna salad. Arrange on a baking sheet (lightly greased or lined with parchment paper). Sprinkle top of each open-face sandwich with about 1 Tablespoon of shredded cheese. Bake at 350° F for about 15 minutes, or until hot through and cheese is melted. Serve at once. Makes 4 to 6.

Cook's Note: These are great topped with a thin slice of tomato. Easy to increase quantities to feed a crowd.

Bar-B-Q Hamburger on Buns

2 pounds hamburger
3/4 cup onion, chopped
2 teaspoons salt
1 Tablespoon chili powder
1 teaspoon pepper
1/2 teaspoon dry mustard
1/3 cup catsup
1 1/3 cups water
2 teaspoons vinegar
1 Tablespoon brown sugar,
    packed
1/3 cup quick-cooking oatmeal
10 hamburger buns

Brown hamburger and onion together in a large saucepan or Dutch oven, breaking up chunks as it cooks. Stir in salt, chili powder, and pepper. Cook 1 or 2 minutes or more. Add dry mustard, catsup, water, vinegar, and brown sugar. Bring to a boil. Add oatmeal, mixing well. Reduce heat; simmer 30 minutes. Serve on hamburger buns. Serves 10.

Cook's Note: See Cooking for a Crowd section for larger quantities.

Pizza Burgers

1 1/2 pounds hamburger
3/4 pound luncheon meat
   (any kind)
1/2 pound American cheese
1 teaspoon salt
1 teaspoon sage
1 Tablespoon oregano
1 1/2 Tablespoons parsley flakes
2 1/2 cups pizza sauce or
   spaghetti sauce
18 hamburger buns

Cook hamburger over medium heat, breaking up chunks as it cooks. Drain off fat. Grind luncheon meat and cheese in meat grinder or food processor. Add to the cooked hamburger, mixing well. Add the remaining ingredients; blend together.

Lay the bottom halves of the buns on baking sheets lined with kitchen parchment paper. Top each half with 1/3 cup meat mixture; lay tops of buns over meat. Cover pan(s) tightly with foil. Bake at 425º F for 12 to 15 minutes, until sandwiches are hot through.

Cook's Note: This is another recipe shared by a short-term worker. Diane Junker (an associate chemistry professor at Milligan College) told us stories about the many years her grandmother cooked for church camps, regularly preparing meals for 100 or more each day. The kids' and staff's favorite lunch was Pizza Burgers. I was so intrigued by the ingredients she remembered that Diane sent me a copy of the recipe when she returned home. (The original serves 100. You'll find that in the Cooking for a Crowd section.)

After a little modification (no American cheese in Austria) we served these at the next conference. The response was overwhelmingly, "Do this again—soon!"

Sloppy Joes

2 1/2 pounds ground beef
1/2 large onion, diced
    (about 3/4 cup)
1/2 medium green pepper, diced
1/2 cup celery, diced
2 Tablespoons brown sugar
2 Tablespoons spicy
    brown mustard
1/2 cup catsup
1/3 cup tomato paste
1 cup tomato sauce
3/4 to 1 cup water
2 Tablespoons vinegar
1 1/2 teaspoons salt (or to taste)
1/4 teaspoon pepper
2 1/2 teaspoons
    Worcestershire sauce
hamburger buns

Cook together the ground beef, onion, green pepper, and celery, breaking up the meat into small pieces as it cooks. Cook until meat is browned and vegetables are transparent. Drain off fat. Add all remaining ingredients, blending well. Cover and simmer about 1 hour, stirring occasionally, until desired consistency. Taste for salt. Serve over split hamburger buns. Serves 10 to 12.

Cook's Note: Another easy lunch-time favorite. Serve with potato chips, plenty of dill pickles, and a tangy make-ahead salad such as Homestead Salad (see Salads and Salad Dressings section)

Hot Dog Wraps

*1/2 of Yeast Dough recipe
    (in this section)
50 LONG hotdogs*

Cook's Note: The all-time favorite lunch menu at Haus Edelweiss is Hot Dog Wraps, Calico Salad, and Potato Chips. Mustard (the brown German type), catsup, and Veggie Trays are provided. Add Peanut Butter Cookies for dessert and we have a Haus-full of happy people.

Allow dough to come to room temperature before starting.

Shape dough into a flattened ball, place on a floured surface and cover with a towel. Allow dough to rest for 5 minutes. Put hot dogs in a pan of hot tap water to warm a bit so they will not chill the dough. When warm, drain and pat dry.

Working on a floured surface, cut dough into 4 pieces; set aside and cover 3 pieces. Roll 1 piece of dough into a rectangle approximately 7x12 inches. With a sharp long-bladed knife cut into strips about 3/4 inches wide. Holding the end of one strip of dough and one end of the hot dog together with a thumb and forefinger, wrap the dough in a spiral down the hot dog. Place 2 to 3 inches apart on lightly greased (or parchment paper lined) baking sheets, being sure that the ends of the dough strips are anchored under each end of the hot dogs.

Cover with a kitchen towel and allow to rise about 1 to 1 1/2 hours in a draft-free, warm place. Bake at 425° for 20 to 25 minutes until golden brown. Check after 20 minutes—you don't want the hot dogs to burst. Remove to platters. Serve at once. Enjoy! Makes about 50 Wraps.

This makes a lot, but try it for a large family picnic or youth group outing. Serves about 25 adults or a dozen hungry teenagers.

Das Brot

Brot (bread) is the only food delivered to Haus Edelweiss. Everything else we serve requires hands-on shopping.

Of the seemingly endless variety of breads available here, four are regularly served at the Haus, but just one—Familientoastbrot (literally "family toast bread")—is pre-sliced and packaged in a plastic wrapper. A square, white bread, firmer than American sandwich breads, it makes wonderful crisp toast. We use it also for Grilled Cheese Sandwiches, Tuna Melts, and Pizza Sandwiches.

The other three—Zeppelin, Pusstawecken, and Gestaubter—arrive in trays, unwrapped and unsliced. Bread is delivered on Mondays and Thursdays during each conference and bread is sliced by kitchen workers using the same kind of slicing machine found in most Austrian homes. Twenty to forty loaves of bread are sliced on an average delivery day; the bread is then placed in plastic bags and stored. These three varieties are served at each meal, with four or five slices of each type in each basket, and more available for refills.

Zeppelin is a medium-soft white loaf in an elongated oval.

Pusstawecken (pronounced POO-shta VECK-en) is an oval Hungarian bread, light tan in color, more dense and with a thicker crust than Zeppelin.

Gestaubter (pronounced ge-SHTOUWB-ter) is a longer, heavy medium-dark rye without caraway seeds. This is the bread most familiar to our Russian and Ukrainian students.

Semmels (pronounced ZIMM-els) are non-sweet rolls, crusty on the outside, soft and fragrant on the inside. They are about four inches in diameter and are commonly used for sandwiches throughout Austria and Germany (where they are known as "Brotchen" or "little bread"). Semmels are served at breakfast on alternate days during conference in place of the usual bread basket. On these days one of the men on staff picks up the freshly-baked Semmels at the Backerei (bakery) in Alland, a small town just five kilometers (3 miles) from the Haus.

Americans who come here agree that Semmels should be sold only with a warning label: "Caution! This product may be addictive!" Wunderbar!

Baking Powder Biscuits

2 cups flour
1 Tablespoon baking powder
1 teaspoon salt
1/2 cup shortening
3/4 cup milk (or a bit less)

Stir together flour, baking powder, and salt. Cut in shortening until mixture resembles coarse meal. With a fork, stir in milk to form a soft, spongy dough. Turn out onto a well-floured surface and knead gently 10 or 12 times. Roll or pat dough to about 1/2 inch thick. Cut into rounds with a floured cutter. Place 1/2 inch apart on a very lightly greased baking pan—or 1 inch apart for crusty sides. Bake at 425 to 450° F for 10 to 12 minutes, until light golden brown. Makes about 12.

Corn Bread

1 cup flour
1 cup yellow corn meal
1/4 cup sugar
1 Tablespoon baking powder
3/4 teaspoon salt
2 eggs
1 cup milk
1/4 cup oil or melted margarine

Combine dry ingredients in a mixing bowl and set aside. In a small bowl, beat eggs; stir in milk and oil. Add liquids to dry ingredients, stirring until all are moistened. Bake in a greased 8-inch square pan at 400° F for 20 to 25 minutes, or until it begins to pull away from the sides of the pan and is very lightly golden brown on top. Cut into 9 squares.

Cook's Note: If you need a larger quantity, 4-times this recipe will yield two 9x13x2 pans. Increase the baking time somewhat. Cut each pan into 18 squares.

Herb Bread

*1 medium loaf
  Italian-style bread
Herb Butter (below)*

Slice bread into 1/2 inch slices. Spread soft Herb Butter on 1 side of each slice, forming it back into its original loaf shape as you work.

Place buttered loaf on a sheet of foil about 6 inches longer than the loaf. Fold sides to the top but do not seal. Fold ends tightly closed to hold the shape of the loaf. Place on a baking sheet; bake at 350° F for about 30 minutes.

Herb Butter

*1 cup margarine, softened
1/8 teaspoon garlic powder
1/4 teaspoon parsley
1/4 teaspoon basil
1/4 teaspoon thyme*

Blend thoroughly. Refrigerate any unused spread, tightly covered. Keeps well.

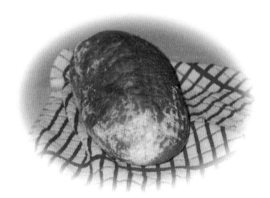

Pussta Bread

Yeast Dough

1 cup water
1/2 cup shortening
1 package dry yeast
1/2 cup lukewarm water
3 eggs
1/2 cup sugar
1 1/2 teaspoons salt
1 cup cold water
8 to 9 cups all-purpose flour

In a 2-cup glass measuring cup, heat the 1 cup of water and the shortening in a microwave until shortening is melted. Set aside to cool. In a small cup, dissolve yeast in the lukewarm water. Break eggs into a large mixing bowl; beat with a fork or whisk to mix. Add the sugar, salt, cold water, yeast mixture, and shortening-water mixture. Stir to dissolve sugar. Add flour 2 cups at a time, stirring to blend well. USE ONLY 8 CUPS OF THE FLOUR to start. Add a little more if needed, until the dough is soft but not sticky. (You will need to use your hands to work in the last half of the flour.) Knead a few times in the bowl until dough is smooth with a satiny look. Place in a LARGE greased stainless steel or glass bowl or a crock. Turn over once to grease the top. Cover with plastic wrap, then lay a kitchen towel over the bowl. Store in refrigerator overnight. (Can be refrigerated up to 3 days but you will need to punch it down once or twice a day.)

When ready to use, punch down the dough, re-cover and bring to room temperature. Turn out onto a floured surface and knead about 12 times, until dough feels elastic and bubbles begin to break the surface. Cut dough in half; cover reserved half. Shape as desired into dinner rolls, Cinnamon Rolls, coffee cake, or Hot Dog Wraps (recipes for Cinnamon Rolls and Hot Dog Wraps are in this section).

This amount of dough will yield about 36 Cinnamon Rolls, or about 50 Hot Dog Wraps.

Cinnamon Rolls

1/2 of Yeast Dough recipe
  (in this section)
4 to 5 Tablespoons very soft
  butter or margarine
1/2 cup sugar
2 teaspoons cinnamon
Glaze (recipe follows)

Combine sugar and cinnamon and set aside.

Working on a lightly floured surface, roll half of the dough into a 10x15 inch rectangle. Spread with soft butter all the way to the edges. Sprinkle with half of the sugar-cinnamon mixture, spreading to the edges with your finger tips or the back of a tablespoon. Beginning along the long side, roll dough up as for a jelly roll. End with seam side down; even up the ends. Cut roll into 1-inch slices using a sharp, thin-bladed knife. Place slices cut side down in a greased 9x13x2 baking pan. Repeat with other half of dough, butter, sugar, and cinnamon. Cover pans with a towel and allow to rise in a warm place until double in bulk (about 1 hour).

Bake at 400° to 425° F for 30 minutes or until very lightly browned on top. Let stand 1 to 2 minutes. Loosen edges and turn out onto a foil-lined baking sheet or tray. Invert onto serving tray (so rolls are right-side up). While still warm, drizzle with a thin glaze. Use 2 forks to gently pull rolls apart for serving. Makes 32 to 36 rolls.

Glaze

1 cup sifted powdered sugar
2 to 3 Tablespoons milk

Stir together to make a thin glaze.

Cook's Note: Cinnamon Rolls are a treat served to short-term workers and staff at break-time on the last Friday of a conference, after their exhausting day of cleaning recently vacated bedrooms and bathrooms, and laundering enough towels and bedding to outfit a small motel.

 Haus Hint: Marti Smith uses a length of dental floss to cut the slices of dough. It does not "squash" them as a knife might. Neat and quick, just slip the piece of floss under one end of the dough, bring the ends up and cross them over, pulling taut so the floss cuts through the dough.

Baked Donut Holes

1 cup sugar
1/4 cup shortening
2 eggs
4 cups flour
4 teaspoons baking powder
1 teaspoon salt
1 teaspoon nutmeg
   (or pumpkin pie spice)
1 cup milk

To coat Donut Holes

1/2 cup margarine, melted
6 Tablespoons sugar
2 Tablespoons cinnamon

Cream together the sugar and shortening until fluffy; add eggs and cream well. Sift together the flour, baking powder, salt, and nutmeg. Add dry ingredients to creamed mixture alternately with milk, beginning and ending with dry ingredients. Grease miniature muffin pans. Drop a rounded teaspoon of batter into each one. Bake at 400º F for 15 to 20 minutes.

While Donut Holes are baking, mix together the sugar and cinnamon in a shallow bowl. When Holes are done, tip them out of the pans onto racks. Brush hot Holes with melted margarine and roll in cinnamon-sugar mixture. Return to rack to cool. (Serve warm—mmm!) Makes about 4 dozen.

Cook's Note: These delightful treats are crunchy on the outside and tender inside. It is impossible to eat just one!

Banana Bread

1 cup sugar
1/2 cup margarine, softened
2 eggs
1 1/2 to 2 cups mashed
     ripe bananas
1 teaspoon lemon juice
1/3 cup milk
2 cups flour
1 teaspoon baking soda
1/2 teaspoon salt
1/2 cup chopped nuts (optional)

Cream margarine and sugar together. Add eggs, bananas, lemon juice, and milk; beat together to blend very well. In a separate bowl, stir together flour, baking soda, salt, and nuts if used. Stir into creamed mixture, blending well. Pour into a greased and floured 9x5 loaf pan. Bake at 350º F for 60 to 70 minutes, or until a wooden pick inserted in the center comes out clean and bread begins to pull away from the sides of the pan. Cool in pan 10 minutes; turn out on a rack and cool completely.

Cook's Note: Banana Bread develops its best flavor if stored, tightly wrapped, for a day or two before cutting.

Haus Hint: The ripest bananas make the best bread. Over-ripe bananas freeze easily for later use. Cut off and discard the stem end, seal bananas in a plastic bag and freeze. When ready to use, thaw on a shallow pan (not a towel; they leave a stain). The skin will be quite dark, but not the banana. Slit the skin and slip the banana out into a measuring cup; break up with a fork.

Chocolate Zucchini Bread

3 eggs
1 cup oil
2 cups sugar
1 Tablespoon vanilla
2 cups shredded zucchini,
*   well packed*
2 1/2 cups flour
1/2 cup cocoa
1 teaspoon salt
1 teaspoon baking soda
1 teaspoon cinnamon
1/4 teaspoon baking powder

Beat together to blend well the eggs, oil, sugar, vanilla, and zucchini. In a separate bowl, combine all of the dry ingredients; stir into liquid mixture to combine thoroughly. Pour into 2 greased 9x5 loaf pans. Bake at 350º F for 1 hour or until a wooden pick inserted in the center comes out clean and bread begins to pull away from the sides of the pan. Cool in pans 10 minutes. Turn out on racks and cool completely. Makes 2 loaves.

Cook's Note: Dark, moist and chocolatey, this is a truly yummy treat. Thanks to my good friend Sara Davisson for sharing.

 Haus Hint: Blessed with an overabundance of zucchini from the garden? Unpeeled shredded zucchini is easy to freeze. Pack firmly into a 2-cup measure and store in small (pint-size) zip-lock freezer bags, flattening package to remove air and make storage easier. Most recipes using shredded zucchini call for 2 cups so to use just thaw and add to the batter you are making. Be sure to include ALL of the "juice" to keep the baked product moist.

Poppy Seed Bread

3 eggs
2 cups sugar
1 cup + 2 Tablespoons oil
3 cups flour
1 1/2 teaspoons salt
1 1/2 teaspoons baking powder
1 1/2 cups milk
1 1/2 teaspoons almond extract
1 1/2 teaspoons vanilla
3 Tablespoons poppy seeds

Glaze (optional)

2 Tablespoons orange juice
1/2 teaspoon almond extract
1/2 teaspoon vanilla
3/4 cup sifted powdered sugar

Beat together eggs, sugar, and oil. In a separate bowl, stir together flour, salt, and baking powder; stir into first mixture, blending well. Add milk, flavorings, and poppy seeds, mixing thoroughly. Pour into 2 well greased and floured 9x5 loaf pans. Bake at 350° F for 1 hour or until a wooden pick inserted in the center comes out clean and bread begins to pull away from the sides of the pan. Cool in pans 10 minutes; turn out on racks to cool completely.

When cool, mix ingredients for glaze until smooth and drizzle on loaves. If you prefer, omit glaze and dust tops of loaves with powdered sugar. Makes 2 loaves.

Cook's Note: A missionary friend in Vienna, Joanne Cooper, shared the recipe for this moist, delicious bread.

Zucchini Bread

3 eggs
2 cups sugar
1 cup oil
1 Tablespoon vanilla
2 cups shredded zucchini,
    packed
2 3/4 cups flour
2 teaspoons baking soda
1/4 teaspoon baking powder
1/4 teaspoon salt
1 Tablespoon cinnamon
1/2 cup chopped nuts (optional)

Beat together the eggs, sugar, and oil; beat in vanilla and zucchini. In a separate bowl, combine flour, baking soda, baking powder, salt, and cinnamon. Stir into liquid mixture 1/3 at a time, mixing well. Stir in nuts if used.

Spray 2 large-size loaf pans with non-stick spray. Cut parchment paper or wax paper to line just the bottom of each pan. Pour batter into the lined pans. Bake at 350º for 1 hour or until a wooden pick inserted in the center comes out clean and bread begins to pull away from the sides of the pan. Cool in pans 10 minutes; turn out on a rack, peel off paper lining, and turn loaves right-side up to cool completely.

Wrap in plastic wrap or store in plastic bags. Freezes very well. Thaw IN BAG before slicing. Flavor is best if bread is allowed to stand overnight. Makes 2 loaves.

Cook's Note: To keep nuts from sinking to the bottom of the batter, remove 1 Tablespoon of the flour mixture before adding dry ingredients to the liquids. Combine the nuts with the 1 Tablespoon of flour mixture before stirring into the batter. A blue ribbon winner at both the Marion County (Indiana) Fair and the Indiana State Fair a number of years ago.

"Thank you very much for your hospitality and your servant spirit. We were never before served and cared for as we were here. It sets a good example for us all. May God bless you and repay you hundred-fold in this life and give you life everlasting in the time to come."

The Polish group

Salads and
Salad Dressings

A Warm Welcome

Hospitality is the hallmark of Haus Edelweiss. Careful attention is given so that "Welcome" is expressed in every detail to all the different language groups.

Spotlessly clean bedrooms and bathrooms, freshly made up with sweet-smelling sheets and fluffy towels, greet new arrivals. A "Welcome bag" containing small toiletries and treats lies on each bed.

Tables in the dining rooms are set with lace-look placemats, and tiny cut-glass vases of fresh flowers grace the tables at every meal. Plates, cups, bowls, and serving dishes of white china bear the Haus Edelweiss logo; flatware is embossed with an edelweiss design. (Edelweiss is the national flower of Austria.) For both dining room and kitchen staffs, presentation is vitally important. Our guests are special people and we want them to know it.

When planning menus, the cook gives thoughtful attention to providing color variety as well as balanced nutrition, and pleasing flavors and textures. Each table of six to eight is hosted by one of the Americans and meals are served family style. Bowls and platters of food are attractively prepared for the most eye-appealing presentation.

For special occasions, as on the final Thursday of each conference, dinner takes on a party air. The dining tables are spread with beautiful placemats woven in a deep green-on-white design (a gift given to the Haus by one of our Hungarian groups). A coordinating napkin, folded in a fan shape, stands at each place and lighted candles cast a warm and intimate glow. The festive meal prepared by the kitchen staff is topped off by an "Ooooh!" inspiring dessert.

This final dinner together is one more way of demonstrating how much each person who comes to Haus Edelweiss is valued and appreciated—to say once more, "We treasure your friendship and are thankful for your dedicated service in your own countries."

Apple-Pineapple Salad

3 medium apples (crisp, red-
  skinned), unpeeled, diced
1 cup pineapple chunks,
  well drained
1/4 cup raisins
1/4 cup walnut pieces (optional)
Jo's Slaw Dressing (below)

Dice apples into a little pineapple juice to prevent darkening. Drain well. Mix the apples, pineapple, and raisins together; add a small amount of dressing to coat fruit. Stir in nuts if used. Serves 8.

Cook's Note: Especially pretty served in a glass bowl.

Haus Hint: To keep apple slices from darkening, drop them into a little pineapple juice and toss to coat. Drain well. This is the only truly effective solution I have found to solve this problem. It works much better than lemon juice, and is effective for banana slices also.

Jo's Slaw Dressing

1 cup real mayonnaise
1/2 cup sugar
1/4 cup vinegar

Beat all ingredients together until sugar is dissolved. Store, tightly covered, in the refrigerator; stir before using. Keeps several weeks. Makes 1 1/4 cups.

Cook's Note: This simple-to-make dressing is so versatile that it works equally well for all creamy cabbage salads, carrot-raisin salad, broccoli salad, and apple salad. Chameleon-like, the flavor suits itself to any of these with a delicious end result.

Creamy Cabbage Salad

4 cups cabbage, shredded
Jo's Slaw Dressing
  (see Apple-Pineapple Salad
  recipe)

Slice cabbage fine in food processor or cut by hand, using a heavy knife, into thin shreds (not chopped fine). Toss with enough dressing to moisten well. Serves 6 to 8.

Cabbage-Apple Salad

3 1/2 cups cabbage, shredded
1 medium red apple,
  unpeeled, diced bite-size
Jo's Slaw Dressing
  (see Apple-Pineapple Salad
  recipe)

Slice cabbage fine in food processor or cut by hand, using a heavy knife, into thin shreds (not chopped fine). Dice apples into a little pineapple juice to prevent darkening. Drain well before adding to cabbage. Toss with enough dressing to moisten. Serves 6 to 8.

Cabbage-Pineapple Salad

Prepare as for Cabbage-Apple salad, substituting 3/4 cup well-drained pineapple chunks for apples.

Peanutty Apple Slaw

3 cups cabbage, finely shredded
2 cups red apple, unpeeled, diced
1/4 cup raisins

Combine dressing ingredients and blend until smooth. Mix with cabbage, apples, and raisins. Serves 6 to 7.

Cook's Note: The dressing gives this crunchy salad its special tang. Try it with Franks and Baked Beans.

Dressing

1/3 cup crunchy peanut butter
  (old-fashioned unhomognized
  is best)
2/3 cup sour cream
3 Tablespoons vinegar
3 Tablespoons orange juice
1 Tablespoon sugar
1/4 teaspoon salt

Carrot-Raisin Salad

*5 to 6 medium carrots, peeled
    and shredded (about 4 cups)*
1/4 cup raisins
*Jo's Slaw Dressing (see Apple-
    Pineapple Salad recipe)*

In a large bowl, combine carrots and raisins. Add enough dressing to moisten well. Serves 6.

Cook's Note: If you like, you can add 1/2 cup well-drained crushed pineapple, which is my daughter-in-law Maggi's favorite addition to this salad.

Haus Hint: To "plump" raisins which have become hard, place in a small bowl and barely cover with a little boiling water. Cover and let stand 5 minutes. Drain well, patting dry with paper towels.

Celery Seed Slaw

7 cups cabbage, shredded
Celery Seed Dressing

Shake or stir dressing ingredients together to dissolve sugar (makes 1 1/2 cups). Mix cabbage with enough dressing to coat well. Serves 8 to 10.

Celery Seed Dressing

3/4 cup cider vinegar
3/4 cup sugar
1 teaspoon salt
1/2 teaspoon celery seed

Sandy's Silly Salad

*16 ounces (4 or 5 cups) cabbage,
    shredded*
6 green onions, sliced (optional)
1/2 cup slivered almonds
2 teaspoons sesame seeds
*2 bags uncooked Ramen noodles,
    chicken flavor*

Dressing

2/3 cup vegetable oil
6 Tablespoons white vinegar
*2 packets chicken-flavor seasoning
    from Ramen noodles*

Put almonds in an ungreased shallow pan and toast lightly in a 350º oven for about 10 minutes, stirring 2 or 3 times. Watch them to prevent over-browning.

Crush the uncooked noodles coarsely. (Use a rolling pin or a meat tenderizer.)

Mix all salad ingredients together. Shake or whisk all dressing ingredients together to mix thoroughly. Toss salad with dressing just before serving. Serves 4 to 6.

Cook's Note: Short-term workers from the States are generous in sharing their recipes. Sadly, some recipes won't work at the Haus because certain ingredients are unavailable or cost prohibitive. This recipe was shared by Sandy Hatfield who also sent along a box of the Ramen noodles! The salad was an instant hit.

Creamy Fruit Salad

*1 can (17 ounces) fruit cocktail
    with juice*
*1 can (20 ounces) pineapple
    chunks, drained (reserve juice)*
*1 can (6 or 8 ounces) mandarin
    oranges, drained*
2 medium bananas, sliced
*1 package (3 ounces) instant
    vanilla pudding*
*1 cup miniature marshmallows
    (optional)**

Combine all ingredients; cover tightly. REFRIGERATE OVERNIGHT. If needed, add a little of the reserved pineapple juice to achieve desired consistency. *Marshmallows are a nice addition, but are not available in Austria. Serves 8 to 10.

Cook's Note: Once she discovered this recipe, it was my mother's favorite dish to take to "Pitch-In" dinners. You can see why: it is easy, MUST be made ahead, and tastes yummy. Also, it is sweet enough to serve as a dessert.

Nutty Bananas

*3 to 4 firm ripe bananas,
   6 to 7 inches long
3 to 4 Tablespoons mayonnaise
1/2 to 3/4 cup finely chopped
   peanuts (cocktail type)
leaf lettuce leaves*

Peel bananas. Put chopped peanuts into a pie pan or similar shallow pan or bowl. Spread each banana with mayonnaise, covering all surfaces. Roll in chopped peanuts to coat completely, pressing gently to keep peanuts in place. Lay on waxed paper or foil until all are coated. Cut each banana into 1-inch chunks using a knife blade dipped in pineapple or lemon juice.

Line serving plate with lettuce leaves; arrange banana chunks on lettuce along with other assorted fruits for an attractive fruit plate. To serve as a salad, line salad plates with a lettuce leaf; arrange 5 or 6 banana chunks on each. Garnish with half a maraschino cherry if desired. If bananas are small, a whole banana may be used for each serving.

Cook's Note: America had not discovered salad bars in the late '30s and early '40s. Salads in the cafeteria of the high school I attended were typical of the era—coleslaw, pickled beets, three-bean salad, potato or macaroni salad, cottage cheese. But two or three times a month, "Banana Salad" would appear on the salad line: half of a banana coated with peanuts nested on a curly leaf of lettuce and topped with a snip of maraschino cherry. What a treat! Years later when I wanted something extra-special to add to a fruit plate I remembered that yummy taste.

Corn Salad

2 cups frozen corn, thawed
    (or drained whole-kernel
    canned corn)
1/2 cup green pepper, diced
1/2 cup celery, diced
1/4 cup onion, finely diced
3/4 cup tomato, diced and
    drained of excess juice
1/4 cup prepared Ranch dressing

Combine all ingredients. Cover and refrigerate 1 hour or more before serving. Serves 8.

Cook's Note: A very colorful and tasty salad, full of garden-fresh vegetables. A delight to the eye as well as the palate.

Haus Hint: To dice onions neatly and easily, peel the onion leaving the root end intact. Cut onion in half top to bottom. Place one half, cut-side down, on a cutting board. Using a medium-size sharp knife and beginning at one cut edge, cut "slices" 1/4 inch apart, working across the curved top side and down to the other edge. Do not cut all the way through the root. Move the knife so it is perpendicular to the original cut and slice again 1/4 inch apart from top to root end. You now have a pile of neat, quarter-inch diced onion.

Green Peas and Cheese Salad

2 packages (10 ounces each)
    frozen peas, thawed
1/2 cup celery, thinly sliced
1/3 cup onion, finely minced
2 cups cheese, cut in small cubes
    (1/2 inch or less)
Dressing

Combine peas, celery, onion, and cheese. Whisk dressing ingredients together to blend thoroughly. Pour over vegetables and cheese; stir well. Chill at least 2 hours before serving. Serves 8 or more.

Cook's Note: Use your favorite cheese. Here at the Haus we use "Holländer Art Käse," a cheese similar to Monterey Jack. Swiss cheese works well also.

Dressing

1/4 cup oil
2 Tablespoons lemon juice
1/8 teaspoon garlic powder
1/2 teaspoon dill weed
1/4 teaspoon crumbled thyme
salt and pepper to taste

Haus Hint: To store peeled onions without perfuming the refrigerator and permanently impregnating the container, always leave the root end intact. Store in a GLASS JAR with a tight fitting lid. Place a folded paper towel in the bottom of the jar. Cover top of jar with plastic wrap before putting on the lid. Avoid storing onion in plastic; plastic is permeable and will absorb and retain the odor.

Mandarin Orange Salad

1 head Bibb lettuce,
    washed and leaves patted dry
1 small can (6 to 8 ounces)
    mandarin orange, drained
2 Tablespoons almond slivers,
    glazed

Dressing

1/4 cup oil
2 Tablespoons sugar
2 Tablespoons vinegar
1/2 teaspoon salt

Shake together in a small jar to blend well and dissolve sugar. Chill.

Glazed Almonds

2 1/4 teaspoons sugar
2 Tablespoons slivered almonds

In a small, heavy skillet combine sugar and almonds. Over medium heat, stir constantly using the flat edge of a heat-proof spatula until almonds are light golden brown. Watch carefully to prevent burning. Remove from the skillet and cool.

At serving time, tear lettuce into bite-size pieces in a large bowl. Toss with dressing (you may not need all of it). Heap into serving bowl and scatter mandarin orange slices and glazed almonds over the top. Toss gently once or twice, being sure to leave some of the oranges and almonds showing on top. Serves 8.

Cook's Note: This truly is NOT complicated, in spite of the three separate sets of instructions. To avoid last-minute fuss: 1) early in the day wash the lettuce, layer the leaves in the folds of a towel, slip into a large plastic bag, and refrigerate; 2) prepare the dressing and refrigerate; 3) glaze almonds and set aside; 4) drain the orange slices and chill. You have only to tear the lettuce and assemble the salad at mealtime. This is THE top favorite salad at Haus Edelweiss.

Sweet and Sour Zucchini Salad

5 cups zucchini, unpeeled
    and thinly sliced
1/2 cup green pepper, diced
1/2 cup celery, diced
1 small onion, sliced paper thin

Dressing

3/4 cup sugar
1 teaspoon salt
1/2 teaspoon pepper
1/2 cup vinegar
1/3 cup oil

Place zucchini, green pepper, celery, and onion in a bowl. Combine dressing ingredients and mix well to dissolve sugar. Pour over vegetables and blend. Cover. REFRIGERATE SEVERAL HOURS OR OVERNIGHT. Serves 8.

Cook's Note: This has become one of the most-requested recipes at the Haus, by both Europeans and Americans.

Fresh Cucumber Salad

3 medium cucumbers,
unpeeled and sliced thin

Dressing

1 cup sugar
3/4 cup water
1/2 cup vinegar
1 teaspoon dried dill weed

Place cucumbers in a bowl or jar with a tight-fitting lid. Whisk dressing ingredients together well (or shake in a jar). Pour over cucumbers and mix together. COVER AND REFRIGERATE SEVERAL HOURS OR OVERNIGHT. Serve with a slotted spoon. Serves 8 to 10.

Cook's Note: Since we serve salads twice daily at Haus Edelweiss, it is a challenge to keep the menu interesting with a wide variety of tasty, nutritious salads during the two weeks of each conference. We are always grateful to those good cooks who share their recipes through magazines. This one came from **Taste of Home.**

Recipe reprinted with permission from **Taste of Home,** *Reiman Publishing*

Kansas Cucumber Salad

*4 medium cucumbers,
    peeled and sliced thin*

Dressing

*1 cup mayonnaise
1/4 cup sugar
1/2 teaspoon salt
1/2 teaspoon dill weed
1/4 teaspoon onion powder
4 teaspoons vinegar*

Mix all dressing ingredients together and combine with cucumber slices in a large bowl. Cover and CHILL IN REFRIGERATOR AT LEAST 1 HOUR. Serves 8.

*Cook's Note: This delicious recipe was adapted from one found in a favorite cookbook (**Taste of Home**) a few years ago.*

*Recipe reprinted with permission from **Taste of Home**, Reiman Publishing*

Macaroni-Pea Salad

*1 1/2 cup uncooked elbow
    macaroni, cooked, rinsed,
    and drained*
1 cup frozen peas, thawed
1/4 cup onion, minced
3/4 cup celery, diced
*1 cup cheddar cheese, cut in
    small cubes (1/2 inch or less)*
1 cup salad dressing or mayonnaise
1/2 teaspoon salt
dash of pepper
1/4 teaspoon Tabasco sauce

Combine the macaroni, peas, onion, celery, and cheese cubes. Mix the remaining ingredients for dressing; fold into macaroni mixture, blending well. Cover. REFRIGERATE OVERNIGHT. Serves 8.

Cook's Note: If mixture seems too stiff at serving time, add a little more salad dressing which has been thinned somewhat with milk.

Rotini Vegetable Salad

1 cup frozen broccoli-cauliflower
    mix, thawed, and drained
    on a towel
1 medium carrot, sliced thin
    and parboiled*
1 small onion (about 1/4 cup)
    cut in paper-thin slices
1 small (4 inch) zucchini,
    thinly sliced
1/4 cup frozen peas, thawed
1 can (4 ounces) sliced
    mushrooms, drained
6 ounces Rotini (spiral
    macaroni), cooked and
    drained

Dressing

1/4 cup mayonnaise
1/4 cup Italian dressing
1/4 cup sour cream
1/4 teaspoon Italian seasoning
dash of pepper

Sprinkle thawed broccoli-cauliflower with salt. Toss together the Rotini and all the vegetables. Mix dressing ingredients, blending well. Pour over pasta mixture; toss to coat well. Taste for salt. Cover and CHILL FOR AT LEAST 1 HOUR. Serves 8 to 10.

*To parboil carrots: in a small saucepan place carrots and just enough water to cover. Bring to a boil over high heat. Cook just 1 minute. Remove from heat; drain and rinse in cold water to stop cooking. Drain again.

Cook's Note: A hearty, flavorful salad. We serve it often for a Sunday evening meal accompanied by a platter of cold cuts and cheese, sliced tomatoes, and a basket of assorted European breads.

Jo's Italian Dressing

1/2 cup vinegar (cider vinegar or white)
1 cup salad oil
1 1/8 teaspoons salt
1/8 teaspoon garlic powder
1/4 teaspoon pepper
3/4 teaspoon dry mustard
1/4 teaspoon Italian seasoning*
1/4 teaspoon basil
1/4 teaspoon onion powder

Whisk together all ingredients until thoroughly blended. Store in a jar with tight-fitting lid. Chill. Makes 1 1/2 cups.

*Italian Herb Seasoning

When your recipe calls for Italian Seasoning and you have none on the shelf this blend will work very well.

2 Tablespoons dried basil
2 Tablespoons dried thyme
2 Tablespoons dried oregano

Crush lightly together. Store in a small jar with a tight lid. Reduce or increase as suits your need, just remember to use equal quantities of each herb.

Chicken Salad with a Twist

6 ounces corkscrew macaroni
1/2 cup Italian dressing
3 cups cooked chicken breast,
*   diced*
1/2 cup mayonnaise
3 Tablespoons lemon juice
1 Tablespoon prepared mustard
1/2 cup onion, very finely diced
1 cup cucumber, peeled and
*   diced*
1 cup celery, thinly sliced or
*   diced*
3/4 cup sliced ripe olives
salt and pepper to taste

Cook macaroni in boiling salted water; drain. AT ONCE add to the hot macaroni the Italian dressing and the chicken. Toss to blend. COOL. Blend together the mayonnaise, lemon juice, mustard, and onion. Add all the remaining ingredients, mixing well. Combine with chicken mixture. Taste for salt. CHILL 2 TO 4 HOURS to blend flavors. Serves 8 to 10.

Cook's Note: After enjoying this flavorful salad at the home of my friend, Carol Hinkley, I knew it should be added to the recipe file in the Haus kitchen. It is served often for Sunday night supper on the first weekend of a conference.

Party Chicken Salad

8 cups cooked chicken breast,
  diced
2 cups celery, diced
1/4 cup onion, minced
1/2 cup (4 ounce can) crushed
  pineapple with juice
2 Tablespoons lemon juice
2 cups real mayonnaise
2/3 cup walnuts, chopped
salt and (white) pepper to taste

Combine chicken, celery, onion, and pineapple. Stir lemon juice into mayonnaise; add to chicken mixture along with walnuts. Blend all together; taste for salt. Cover. CHILL SEVERAL HOURS OR OVERNIGHT to blend flavors. Serves 12 to 16.

Cook's Note: My favorite chicken salad. This, like Potato Salad, needs a little time for flavors to "marry." If you like, you may add 1/2 cup halved seedless green grapes.

Turkey Salad

4 cups cooked turkey breast, diced

3 eggs, hard cooked and diced

1 cup celery, diced

1/2 cup dill pickle, diced

1 small crisp apple, peeled and diced fine or shredded

1 cup mayonnaise

2 teaspoons onion, minced

1 teaspoon lemon juice

1 teaspoon salt

1/8 teaspoon pepper

Combine the turkey, eggs, celery, dill pickle, and apple in a large bowl. Blend mayonnaise, onion, lemon juice, salt, and pepper. Pour over turkey mixture; blend thoroughly. If necessary, add a little more mayonnaise. Taste for salt. CHILL SEVERAL HOURS OR OVERNIGHT. Serves 8.

Cook's Note: A Sunday evening favorite at Haus Edelweiss.

Calico Salad

*2 1/2 cups (29 ounce can) green
    beans, drained*
*2 1/2 cups (29 ounce can) whole
    kernel corn, drained*
*4 cups (40 ounces) canned red
    kidney beans, drained
    and rinsed*
1 1/2 Tablespoons onion, minced
1/2 cup green pepper, diced

Dressing

1 cup sugar
1/2 cup oil
1/2 cup vinegar

Combine vegetables in a large bowl. Whisk dressing ingredients together in a bowl until sugar is dissolved. Pour over vegetables and mix well. Place in a covered container and REFRIGERATE OVERNIGHT to marinate. Stir well before serving. Makes about 8 cups (10 to 12 servings).

Cook's Note: Serve with a slotted spoon to drain off excess marinade. This keeps a week or more in the refrigerator. A lunch-time favorite at the Haus.

Homestead Salad

2 packages (10 ounces each)
  frozen mixed vegetables
1 rib celery, diced
1/2 medium green pepper, diced
1/2 cup onion, finely diced
1 can (20 ounces) kidney beans,
  drained and rinsed

Dressing

3/4 cup sugar
3 Tablespoons flour
1 teaspoon dry mustard
1/2 cup vinegar

Cook mixed vegetables in boiling salted water until tender-crisp; drain. Combine with other vegetables. Blend sugar, flour, and dry mustard in a saucepan. Stir in vinegar, taking care to avoid lumping. Cook over medium heat, stirring constantly, until mixture thickens and boils. Lower heat; cook 1 or 2 minutes longer. Pour hot dressing over all and blend well. Place in a covered container and REFRIGERATE OVERNIGHT to marinate. Stir well before serving. Serves 8 to 10.

Haus Hint: After peeling or chopping onion, rub the bowl of a stainless steel spoon over every surface of your fingers and hands. Wash your hands with soap and water. The smell is gone. Honest! (Even a chemist was baffled as to why this works. It just DOES.)

Sauerkraut Salad

1 can (29 ounces) sauerkraut
1 cup celery, diced
1/2 cup onion, finely diced
3/4 cup green pepper, diced

Dressing

1 cup sugar
1/3 cup oil
1/3 cup vinegar

Rinse sauerkraut very thoroughly to remove brine; drain well. Combine with celery, onion, and green pepper. Shake dressing ingredients together in a jar or whisk in a bowl to dissolve sugar. Pour dressing over vegetables; mix well. Cover; REFRIGERATE OVERNIGHT or longer to marinate. Serves 8.

Cook's Note: This keeps very well and the flavors improve with standing. We try to make it 2 or 3 days ahead for that reason. Even people who claim not to like sauer-kraut respond enthusiastically when this tangy, unusual salad is served.

Jo's Potato Salad

8 medium white potatoes, peeled
1 1/3 cups celery, diced
1/3 cup dill pickle, diced
2 to 3 Tablespoons onion,
    minced
1/4 teaspoon celery salt
1 1/4 cups real mayonnaise
1 Tablespoon prepared mustard
6 eggs, hard-cooked and diced
    (reserve 4 or 5 slices)
salt and pepper to taste

Dice potatoes bite-size; cook in salted water until just tender. Drain in a colander, shaking gently to dry a bit. Place hot potatoes in a bowl and at once add celery, dill pickle, onion, and celery salt. Mix gently. Combine mayonnaise and mustard; pour over vegetables. Add diced eggs and mix gently to combine and coat potatoes thoroughly. Turn into a serving dish and garnish with reserved egg slices. If desired, dust with a little paprika. Cover. CHILL SEVERAL HOURS OR OVERNIGHT. Serves 8 to 10.

Cook's Note: Some foods take a little time to develop their best flavors, and potato salad is one of these. It is definitely better the second day. Leftovers keep well.

Jesus said, "He who would be greatest among you must be the servant of all." Students who come to Haus Edelweiss for training tell us that their lives are influenced here as much by the servant leadership they see modeled as by what they learn in the classroom. For example, the sight of their professors drying dishes in the kitchen amazes them. They say, "In my country this would not happen."

"And the King will reply, 'I tell you the truth, whatever you did for one of the least of these brothers of mine, you did for me'" (Matthew 25:40).

Entrees
Main Dishes

The Gift of Service

Service—true service—in the way Jesus used the word, is to give of oneself: freely, gladly, generously, without needing or expecting recognition or reward. A radical concept in many areas of our world today where the basic mind-set leans more toward satisfying one's own desires. But there are many who have learned the joy and contentment that service such as this can bring into their lives. That attitude blesses the work and daily life of Haus Edelweiss. Some very special folks come to mind, notably short-term workers (STWs) and professors.

In a class by themselves, the STWs who come to serve for two weeks at Haus Edelweiss are a heaven-sent gift. Paying their own airfare and using vacation days from work, or coming on their own time, the groups arrive from all over the United States. More than 100 of them will serve during the course of a year. Each one is aware that this will not be a vacation in the ordinary sense of the word. By the time they leave Austria to return home, "servanthood" will have taken on a whole new meaning.

Working alongside staff, they help with meal preparation, set tables, mop floors, clean bathrooms, and launder mountains of towels and bedding. Some mow lawns, sweep sidewalks, plant flowers, rake leaves, paint buildings. Willing hands help out wherever they are needed or assigned. The work day is long, sometimes ten hours or more, and the work is hard. Maintaining six buildings inside and out and tending six and a half acres of hilly, wooded property are not easy tasks. Nor is preparing three meals daily for 85 to 95 hungry Europeans and Americans. Yet a comment we frequently hear is, "This has been the most rewarding experience of my life."

And there are the professors. TCM is blessed by the committed service of more than two dozen respected teachers and administrators. They teach in the classrooms at the Haus Edelweiss campus, or travel in-country to teach at one of the ten training centers TCM has established in Central and Eastern Europe.

The love and dedication of those who help and serve in every area at Haus Edelweiss lift and encourages everyone who comes here. Their energy and enthusiasm infuse the property with joy. The ministry of TCM exists and is effective because of the willing spirits of those who give so much of themselves.

Baked Beef and Rigatoni

1 pound lean ground beef
1/2 cup onion, chopped
1/3 cup green pepper, diced
3 cups canned Italian style
    tomatoes, cut up
1 cup (8 ounce can) tomato
    sauce
3/4 cup (6 ounce can) tomato
    paste
3/4 cup water
1 can (4 ounces) sliced mush-
    rooms (with juice)
1/8 teaspoon garlic powder
2 teaspoons sugar
1 teaspoon oregano
1 1/2 teaspoons salt
1/4 teaspoon pepper
1 1/2 teaspoons parsley flakes
2 eggs, slightly beaten
1 cup (8 ounce carton) cottage
    cheese
1/2 cup Parmesan cheese, grated
6 ounces Rigatoni, cooked and
    drained

Cook together the ground beef, onion, and green pepper, breaking up meat as it cooks, until meat is done and onion transparent. Add tomatoes, tomato sauce, tomato paste, water, mushrooms with juice, and all the seasonings. Bring to a boil. Lower heat and simmer one hour. Remove from heat.

Cook Rigatoni in boiling, salted water. Drain and KEEP HOT.

In a large bowl mix together the beaten eggs, cottage cheese and Parmesan cheese. Add the hot cooked Rigatoni and mix together thoroughly. Spoon mixture into a greased 9x13x2 baking dish. Top with tomato-meat sauce. Bake at 350° F for 45 to 60 minutes or until heated through. If desired, sprinkle with some additional Parmesan cheese. Serves 8 to 10.

Lasagna

5 cups Italian Meat Sauce
     (recipe follows)
10 ounces lasagna noodles,
     not cooked
1 cup small curd cottage cheese
1/3 cup grated Parmesan cheese
1/4 cup milk
3 to 3 1/2 cups shredded
     Mozzarella cheese

Combine the cottage cheese, Parmesan cheese, and milk in a bowl. Let stand 5 minutes or so to thicken.

Spray a 9x13x2 baking pan with non-stick vegetable spray. Ladle about 1/2 cup of the sauce into the pan, spreading evenly. Place a layer of the uncooked noodles in the pan, breaking and fitting as needed to cover the bottom. Dot noodles with one third of the cottage cheese mixture. Ladle on about 1 1/2 cups of sauce; sprinkle with about 1 cup of Mozzarella.

Repeat twice, making three layers. Use a little more sauce and a little more cheese on the top layer.

Cover tightly with foil. Bake at 350° F for 1 1/2 to 2 hours, removing foil during the last 20 minutes. Let stand at least 10 minutes before cutting into 12 servings (3x3 inch squares). Serves 8 to 10.

Cook's Note: This is the hands-down favorite casserole served at Haus Edelweiss to any group and is served at most conferences. It seems to be a special favorite of Polish and Hungarian students.

Italian Meat Sauce

Meat mixture

1 pound ground beef
1/2 cup diced onion
1 teaspoon salt
1/4 teaspoon pepper
1/8 teaspoon garlic powder

Sauce

3 1/2 cups (24 ounce can)
   Italian-style tomatoes, cut up
3/4 cup (6 ounce can) tomato paste
1 cup (8 ounce can) tomato sauce
1 cup water
3/4 teaspoon sugar
1/2 teaspoon basil
1/2 teaspoon oregano
3/4 teaspoon parsley flakes
1/4 teaspoon garlic powder
salt (to taste)

In a large heavy pot, cook the ground beef and onion until onion is transparent, breaking up meat as it cooks. Season with the salt, pepper, and 1/8 teaspoon garlic powder. Add all the rest of the ingredients and combine well. Bring to a boil; lower heat and simmer, covered, one hour, stirring occasionally. Taste for seasonings; adjust to your personal liking. If necessary, continue to simmer until desired consistency is reached. Serve over spaghetti.

Cook's Note: This recipe makes enough sauce for one 9x13x2 pan of lasagna. For lasagna, the sauce needs to be thinner than for serving over spaghetti because the lasagna noodles are not pre-cooked. Large quantities will, of course, require longer cooking.

Meatloaf

2 eggs
2/3 cup milk
1 teaspoon salt
1/2 teaspoon dry parsley flakes
1/4 teaspoon onion powder
1/4 teaspoon pepper
2/3 cup fine dry bread crumbs
2 1/4 pounds hamburger

In a large bowl, beat eggs. Add milk and seasonings; stir in bread crumbs. Let stand a few minutes to absorb liquids. Add hamburger and mix thoroughly, using your nice clean hands.

Form into a loaf shape, patting and shaping firmly so it will hold its shape. Place in a shallow baking pan, laying a sheet of foil loosely over the top. Bake at 350° F for 1 3/4 hours. Remove foil during last half hour.

Let stand in the pan 10 minutes before removing and slicing. Serves 8.

Cook's Note: If you prefer, mixture can be packed into a 9x5x3 loaf pan and baked for same time.

Mini Bar-B-Q Meatloaves

Recipe for Meat Loaf in this
*   section*
2 cups Bar-B-Q Sauce
*   (recipe follows)*

Prepare recipe for Meat Loaf. Divide mixture into 8 equal portions. Form each portion into a loaf shape. Arrange loaves in a shallow pan (or baking sheet with sides). Top each loaf with approximately 1/4 cup Bar-B-Q sauce. Bake uncovered at 350° F about 1 hour. Serve with extra sauce if desired. Serves 8.

Bar-B-Q Sauce

2 cups catsup
1/4 cup cider vinegar
1/2 teaspoon salt
1/8 teaspoon pepper
1/8 teaspoon onion powder
1 1/2 teaspoons sugar
1/2 teaspoon Worcestershire
*   sauce*
1/8 teaspoon chili powder
1 1/2 teaspoons lemon juice
1/2 cup water

Blend all ingredients together. Heat together but do not boil. (Heating helps to blend flavors.) Makes about 2 3/4 cups.

Cook's Note: Substitute your favorite bottled Bar-B-Q sauce if you like. Quantities are easy to divide for a small family. This has always been a favorite of my family and it tastes just as good today as when I first tried the recipe in 1943. Great served with baked potatoes, green beans, and a salad.

Sweet and Sour Meat Balls

*Recipe for Meat Loaf in this
   section*
*1 cup pineapple chunks, drained
   (reserve juice)*
*1/2 cup green pepper, cut in
   1/4 to 1/2 inch wide strips*
*Sweet and Sour Sauce (see Sweet
   and Sour Turkey recipe)*

Prepare recipe for Meat Loaf; shape mixture into balls 1 to 1 1/2-inches in diameter. Roll in your hands to make them firm. Arrange meatballs in a 9x13x2 baking pan. Bake at 400° F for about 15 minutes. Drain off all fat. Lower oven temperature to 350° F.

Scatter pineapple chunks and green pepper over meat balls; pour Sweet and Sour Sauce over the top. Cover pan with foil; bake for another 40 to 45 minutes. Serve over rice or noodles. Serves 8.

Norwegian Meatballs

1 egg
1/2 cup milk
1/2 cup dry bread crumbs
1/4 cup onion, minced
1 teaspoon salt
1 teaspoon sugar
1/4 teaspoon ginger
1/4 teaspoon nutmeg
1/4 teaspoon allspice
1/8 teaspoon pepper
1 1/2 pounds ground beef
Gravy (recipe below)

In a large bowl stir together all ingredients except the meat. Let stand a few minutes until milk is absorbed. Add meat and mix thoroughly. Shape into 1 inch balls; place in a shallow baking pan. Bake at 400° F, 18 to 20 minutes until browned. Drain off fat. Set aside.

Gravy

1 1/2 Tablespoons margarine
1 Tablespoon onion, minced
2 1/2 Tablespoons flour
2 cups beef broth
1/4 cup heavy cream
*   (or evaporated milk)*
dash of cayenne pepper
dash pepper

In a skillet, sauté onion in margarine over medium heat until tender. Stir in flour and brown lightly. Slowly add broth, stirring constantly with a whisk until smooth and thickened. Blend in cream, cayenne, and pepper. Gently stir in meatballs. Heat through but do not boil. Serves 8.

Porcupine Meat Balls

1 pound ground beef
1/2 cup water
1/3 cup onion, finely minced
1/2 teaspoon salt
1 teaspoon celery salt
1/8 teaspoon garlic powder
1/8 teaspoon pepper
1/2 cup uncooked rice

Sauce

2 cups tomato sauce
1 cup water
2 teaspoons Worcestershire sauce

Mix together thoroughly the meat, water, onion, seasonings, and rice. Shape into balls, using a rounded Tablespoon of mixture for each one. Place in a 2-quart baking dish. Do not crowd.

Mix sauce ingredients and pour over meat balls. Cover tightly with foil. Bake at 350° F for 45 minutes; uncover and bake 15 minutes longer. Serves 4 to 6.

Cook's Note: This is so easy because it is all done in the oven—no separate browning of the meatballs. Thanks for this recipe goes to my sister, Helen, who many years ago gave me a collection of recipes assembled by Owen County, Indiana, Homemakers Clubs. Lots of good cooks in Indiana!

Spaghetti Pie

1 pound ground beef
1/2 cup onion, chopped
2 cups spaghetti sauce (store
_   bought or your own)_
7 ounces thin spaghetti
2 Tablespoons margarine, melted
1/3 cup grated Parmesan cheese
2 eggs, beaten
1 cup small curd cottage cheese
1/2 cup shredded Mozzarella
_   cheese_

Brown ground beef and onion together, breaking up meat as it cooks. Drain off fat. Stir meat into spaghetti sauce; set aside.

Meanwhile, cook spaghetti as directed on package; drain. To the HOT spaghetti add melted butter, Parmesan cheese, and beaten eggs, tossing well to coat evenly. Pour mixture into a greased 10-inch pie pan, shaping it up the sides to form a crust.

Spread cottage cheese over just the bottom of the crust, not up to the top edge. Pour meat sauce mixture over all and spread evenly, again leaving top edge of crust uncovered. Bake at 350° F for 20 to 25 minutes. Sprinkle with Mozzarella cheese; bake 5 minutes more to melt cheese. Cool for 10 minutes before cutting in wedges to serve. Serves 6 to 7.

Cook's Note: Two cups of your own home-made meat sauce may be substituted for the store-bought sauce, meat, and onion. This, in fact, is the way we prepare it at the Haus in Austria.

My niece, Libby Noll, makes this for family get-togethers—the recipe multiplied many times and baked in a huge pan. Thanks for sharing, Libby.

Chicken-Broccoli Bake

5 cups (24 ounces) frozen
   chopped broccoli
5 cups cooked chicken breast,
   diced
2 cans cream of chicken soup,
   undiluted
2 teaspoons lemon juice
1 cup mayonnaise
1/2 teaspoon curry powder
1/2 cup fine, fresh bread crumbs
   (1 slice, crusts removed)
1 cup shredded cheddar cheese

Cook broccoli until just tender-crisp; drain well. Place in bottom of a greased 9x13x2 baking dish. Scatter chicken over broccoli.

In a bowl, combine the chicken soup, lemon juice, mayonnaise, and curry powder, blending well. Pour over chicken, spreading evenly. Sprinkle crumbs over sauce; cover all with the cheddar cheese. Bake at 350° F, 35 to 40 minutes, until cheese is melted and mixture is hot and bubbly. Serves 8 to 10.

Cook's Note: This can be prepared a day ahead and refrigerated. Remove an hour or two before baking; increase baking time as needed.

Primarily a meat-and-potatoes man for the first half of our long life together, my husband took a dim view of meals served in a casserole. Asked to explain his obvious enjoyment of this particular dish, he blandly replied that it didn't "taste like a casserole" to him, therefore it wasn't a casserole.

Chicken Noodle Parmesan

1/3 cup margarine
4 Tablespoons flour
1 1/2 cups chicken broth
1 cup milk
1/2 cup evaporated milk
1/2 teaspoon salt
1/4 teaspoon pepper
1 can (4 ounces) sliced
    mushrooms, drained
2 1/2 to 3 cups cooked, diced
    chicken
1 cup grated Parmesan cheese,
    DIVIDED
8 ounces medium noodles,
    cooked and drained
paprika

To prepare sauce, melt margarine in a pan, stir in flour and mix until smooth. Add chicken broth, stirring constantly. Continue stirring while adding milk, evaporated milk, salt, and pepper. Bring to a boil; lower heat and simmer one minute. Remove from heat. Taste for seasonings. Stir in mushrooms, chicken, 3/4 cup of the Parmesan cheese, and the noodles.

Place in a greased 9x13x2 baking dish. Sprinkle with remaining Parmesan cheese and a little paprika. Bake at 400° F for 20 minutes until hot and bubbly. Serves 8.

Chicken Pot Pie

12 Baking Powder Biscuits
(see Soups, Sandwiches,
and Breads section for
recipe)

1/4 cup margarine
1/2 cup flour
4 cups rich chicken stock
1/4 teaspoon onion powder
(optional)
salt and pepper to taste
3 cups cooked chicken, diced
3/4 cup diced carrots, cooked
1/2 cup frozen peas

Pre-heat oven to 425° F.

Prepare Baking Powder Biscuits, cover and set aside.

In a saucepan, melt margarine over medium heat. Blend in flour (and onion powder, if used). Gradually stir in chicken stock, cooking and stirring until smooth and thickened. Lower heat and cook gently for about two minutes. Add chicken, carrots, and peas. Cook a few minutes longer until mixture is piping hot. Pour into a greased 9x13x2 baking dish.

Immediately lay twelve Baking Powder Biscuits on top of hot mixture. Place in pre-heated oven. Bake 15 to 20 minutes, or until biscuits are golden brown and cooked through, and mixture bubbles around them. Serves 8 to 10.

Cook's Note: Real comfort food. I like to mix extra biscuit dough and bake a pan full to serve along with the pot pies. Be sure to have some honey or your favorite jam available.

Chicken Rice Casserole

1/3 cup margarine
1/3 cup onion, finely diced
1/3 cup celery, finely diced
1/3 cup flour
3/4 teaspoon salt
1 1/3 cups chicken broth
1 cup milk
1 cup evaporated milk
3 cups cooked chicken breast,
    diced
2 cups cooked rice
1 can (4 ounces) mushrooms,
    drained and chopped
1 cup shredded cheese
2/3 cup rich cracker crumbs

Sauté onion and celery in margarine until transparent. Add flour and salt, cooking and stirring briefly to blend. Gradually add chicken broth, blending well; cook and stir until it bubbles. Add milk and evaporated milk in the same manner, stirring often to prevent sticking. When mixture comes to a boil, lower heat and simmer one minute. Remove from heat and stir in mushrooms, chicken, and rice.

Spoon mixture into a greased 7x11 baking dish. Sprinkle top with shredded cheese and crumbs. Bake at 350° F until hot through and bubbly at edges (about 30 to 45 minutes). Serves 6 to 8.

Cook's Note: Another very popular dish at the Haus. The only way to assure leftovers is to make an extra casserole! A legacy from a former cook.

Herbed Chicken Casserole

1/2 cup margarine
1/2 cup onion, chopped
1/2 cup celery, chopped
8 ounce package Pepperidge
    Farm Herb Stuffing Mix*
1 cup warm water
2 1/2 cups cooked chicken, diced
1/2 cup mayonnaise
3/4 teaspoon salt
1/4 teaspoon pepper
2 eggs, beaten
1 1/2 cups milk
1 can cream of mushroom soup,
    undiluted
1 cup shredded cheese

Sauté onion and celery in margarine until vegetables are limp. Add stuffing mix and water; blend well. Put half of the mixture in the bottom of a 9x13x2 baking dish. Mix together the chicken, mayonnaise, salt, and pepper. Spread over stuffing in pan. Top with rest of stuffing mixture. In a separate bowl, combine beaten eggs and milk. Carefully pour over ingredients in baking dish. Cover with plastic wrap. REFRIGERATE OVERNIGHT.

Remove from refrigerator one hour or more before time to bake. Spread the undiluted mushroom soup over the top. Bake uncovered at 325° F for about 45 minutes or until hot through. Sprinkle with shredded cheese. Bake 10 minutes longer. Serves 8 to 10.

Cook's Note: This casserole can be frozen before baking. Thaw completely before spreading with mushroom soup. Bake as directed. My friend Elaine Schultz serves this recipe and calls it "Chicken Normandy."

*Prepared Herb Stuffing Mix is not available in Austria, but when a really good recipe is at stake the creative cooks who have served at Haus Edelweiss have usually viewed this as just another challenge. Following is the substitute herb stuffing mixture used at the Haus:

Haus Special Stuffing Mix

1 bag (227 grams) vollkorn
Krisp Rolls, crushed with
a rolling pin
2 to 3 teaspoons Kräuter der
Provence seasoning
1/2 teaspoon salt
1/4 teaspoon pepper
1/4 to 1/2 teaspoon regular
poultry seasoning

Stir together to mix well. Taste for seasoning.

Cook's Note: Kräuter der Provence is a savory seasoning blend containing basil, rosemary, marjoram, oregano, parsley, and thyme. We often use it to season pork shoulder roast also. The Krisp Rolls are similar to rusks—a dry, hard-bread product. (Vollkorn means whole grain or whole wheat.)

Oven-Easy Chicken

Boneless, skinless chicken breast halves are the greatest boon to the busy cook since cake mixes. The ways to prepare them are as endless as your imagination. The very simplest require only dipping the chicken breasts in some liquid— melted margarine, milk, or a simple egg wash (1 egg beaten with 1/4 cup water), then dredging in a flavorful coating. Bake at 375° F for 45 minutes or until chicken is tender and crispy on the outside. What could be easier?

Four favorites, served regularly at Haus Edelweiss, are included here. The Cheezy version, passed on to me by my sister Helen, I prepare only on the other side of the Atlantic. (Although the cheese crackers can sometimes be found in Austria, they are cost-prohibitive for the quantities we serve here.) But it is too good to omit.

Two of the coatings can be prepared in quantity and stored air-tight to have on hand when time is short—yet another busy-day help. These recipes are found in this section.

Be creative! Experiment with your own favorite herbs and spices. Try crushed cornflakes or any flavorful snack cracker, crushed for a crunchy coating. Remember, every "new" recipe is the result of some cook's successful experiment.

Quantities have not been specified for any of these Oven-Easy recipes because you can prepare as few or as many as you desire. Six chicken breast halves will serve 4 to 6 persons, depending upon appetites. Remember, if you are baking multiple pans of chicken at one time, a little extra baking time may be required.

Another tip: for easy clean-up, line baking pans with kitchen parchment baking paper.

Oven "Fried" Chicken

Pat chicken breasts dry. Dip in milk or water; dredge in Basic Breading Mix (recipe follows). Place, a little apart, on a shallow baking sheet lined with kitchen parchment paper. Bake at 375° F for about 45 minutes or until chicken is tender.

Basic Breading Mix

5 cups dry, fine bread crumbs
1 1/2 teaspoons salt
1 1/2 teaspoons paprika
1 1/2 teaspoons celery salt
1/2 teaspoon pepper
1/3 cup vegetable oil

Mix together thoroughly. Store air-tight. Needs no refrigeration; keeps well. Makes 5 1/4 cups.

Oven Ranch Chicken

Pat chicken breasts dry. Dip in melted margarine. Lay on a shallow baking sheet lined with kitchen parchment paper. Sprinkle generously with dry Ranch Dressing mix—regular or Honey Dijon. Bake at 350° F for 45 to 55 minutes or until chicken is tender.

Cook's Note: Ranch Dressing mix is not available in Austria but our kind and generous short-term workers tuck packets in their suitcases to keep us supplied.

Easy Cheezy Chicken

Pat chicken breasts dry. Dip in melted margarine; roll in finely crushed cheddar cheese cracker crumbs (such as Cheez-Its). Lay a little apart on a shallow baking pan lined with kitchen parchment paper. Bake at 350° F for 45 to 55 minutes or until chicken is tender and outside is crunchy. Delicious!

Parmesan Chicken

Pat chicken breasts dry. Dip in an egg-wash (1 egg beaten with 1/4 cup water). Dredge in Parmesan Breading Mix (recipe follows). Lay on a shallow baking sheet lined with kitchen parchment paper. Bake at 375° F for about 45 minutes or until chicken is tender.

Parmesan Breading Mix

3 cups fine, dry bread crumbs
3 cups grated Parmesan cheese
1 Tablespoon parsley flakes, crushed
1 Tablespoon salt
1 teaspoon pepper
3/4 teaspoon garlic powder

Mix thoroughly. Refrigerate stored in an air-tight container. Makes 6 cups.

Crispy Parmesan Chicken

Pat chicken breasts dry. Mix equal quantities of Parmesan Breading Mix (see Parmesan Chicken recipe) and finely crushed cornflake crumbs.

Dip chicken in melted margarine then dredge in the Parmesan-cornflake mixture, coating well. Place a little apart on a shallow baking sheet lined with kitchen parchment paper. Bake at 375° F for about 45 minutes or until chicken is tender and nice and crispy on the outside.

Cook's Note: At Haus Edelweiss, this is the top favorite way to serve chicken breasts.

Scalloped Chicken

3 eggs
3 cups chicken broth
2 Tablespoons onion, finely
minced
3/4 cup celery, diced
10 slices white bread, cut in 1
inch cubes
1 cup saltine cracker crumbs
1 teaspoon salt
3 cups cooked chicken, diced
1 can (4 ounces) mushrooms,
drained and chopped
1 Tablespoon melted margarine
1/2 cup lightly crushed rich
crackers (such as Ritz)

In a large bowl beat eggs slightly. Stir in chicken broth, onion, celery, bread, saltine cracker crumbs, and salt. Mix together and add chicken and mushrooms, blending well. Let stand 10 minutes.

Spoon into a greased 2-quart (7x11) baking dish. Combine the 1/2 cup rich cracker crumbs and melted margarine; sprinkle over top. Bake at 350° F for about 1 hour or until a table knife blade inserted in the center comes out clean. Let stand 10 to 15 minutes to set before serving. Serves 6 to 8.

Cook's Note: A "keeper" from **Taste of Country** *magazine.*

Recipe reprinted with permission from **Taste of Country,** *Reiman Publishing*

Ham and Cheese Strata

8 cups firm white bread, cut in
   1/2 inch cubes
2 cups cooked ham, cut in 1/2
   inch cubes
3 cups shredded Monterey Jack
   cheese
5 eggs
2 cups milk
1 cup evaporated milk
1 teaspoon dry mustard
1/4 teaspoon onion powder
1/4 teaspoon salt
1 1/2 cups finely crushed
   cornflakes
1/3 cup melted margarine

In the bottom of a 9x13x2 baking dish, layer half of the bread, half of the ham, and half of the cheese. Repeat layers with remaining bread, ham, and cheese. In a bowl, beat the eggs well. Add milk, evaporated milk, and seasonings, mixing thoroughly. Carefully pour mixture over contents of baking dish. Sprinkle cornflake crumbs over the top; drizzle melted margarine over crumbs. Cover with plastic wrap. REFRIGERATE OVERNIGHT.

Remove from refrigerator an hour or two before you are ready to bake. Bake at 375° F for 45 to 50 minutes or until a table knife inserted in center comes out clean. Let stand at least 10 minutes before cutting to allow strata to "set." Serves 8 to 10.

Cook's Note: To more readily dissolve dry mustard and onion powder, place them in a small cup along with the salt and add two teaspoons hot water. Blend well. Add to the egg and milk mixture.

Often great-sounding recipes found in magazines need to be adapted to be workable at Haus Edelweiss. This is one of those. American style ham is not readily available in Austria. We found we could use the deli-type "ham" sandwich meat sold in loaf form. Not quite the same flavor, but a very satisfactory result. Our students of all nationalities really enjoy this dish served for lunch or dinner.

Tuna at its Best

1 can cream of mushroom soup,
    undiluted
1/2 cup milk
1/2 cup mayonnaise
1/4 teaspoon onion powder
1/8 teaspoon pepper
1 can (6 3/4 - 7 ounces) chunk
    tuna, drained
1/2 cup Monterey Jack cheese,
    shredded
1 can (4 ounces) mushrooms,
    drained and chopped
    (optional)
1/2 cup frozen peas, thawed
6 ounces medium noodles,
    cooked and drained
3/4 cup crushed potato chips

In a large bowl mix thoroughly the mushroom soup, milk, mayonnaise, onion powder, and pepper. Blend in tuna, cheese, mushrooms, and peas. Add the cooked, drained noodles and toss to combine thoroughly.

Spread mixture in a greased 2-quart (7x11) baking dish. Top with crushed potato chips. Bake at 350° F for 30 to 40 minutes or until hot throughout. Serves 6 to 7.

Cook's Note: For a bit more crunch and nice change of taste, you may substitute 1/2 cup slivered almonds for the crushed potato chip topping.

Sweet and Sour Turkey

*2 pounds boneless, skinless
    turkey breast*
*1 cup pineapple chunks, drained
    (reserve juice)*
*1/2 cup green pepper strips, cut
    1/4 inch wide*
*Sweet and Sour Sauce (recipe
    follows)*

Cut turkey breasts into finger-size strips; place in the bottom of a 9x13x2 baking pan. Scatter pineapple chunks and green pepper strips over the top of turkey. Pour sauce over all. Cover pan with foil; bake at 350° F for one hour. Uncover and bake 10 minutes longer. Serve over hot fluffy rice. Serves 8 to 10.

Sweet and Sour Sauce

3/4 cup + 1 Tablespoon catsup
1/3 cup cider vinegar
1/4 cup brown sugar, packed
*1/2 cup pineapple juice (drained
    from pineapple)*
1 3/4 Tablespoons cornstarch
1 teaspoon soy sauce

Combine all ingredients in a saucepan. Cook over medium heat, stirring until mixture comes to a boil. Lower heat, cooking a few minutes longer until sauce thickens and clears. Makes about 1 1/2 cups.

Cook's Note: This sauce works equally well for Sweet and Sour Turkey and for Sweet and Sour Meatballs.

Turkey Stir Fry

*3/4 pound turkey breast, cut in
    bite-size pieces*
*Oil for cooking meat and
    vegetables*
3/4 cup onion, sliced very thin
2 ribs celery, sliced diagonally
*1 small zucchini (about 4 inches
    long), sliced*
*16 ounces frozen broccoli-cauli-
    flower-carrot mix, thawed
    and patted dry*
*4 ounce can mushroom slices,
    drained (reserve liquid)*
3/4 cup chicken broth
*2 to 4 Tablespoons soy sauce
    (to taste)*
2 teaspoons sugar
1 Tablespoon cornstarch
*3 Tablespoons liquid from
    mushrooms*

In a large heavy skillet, over medium-high heat, cook turkey pieces in a small amount of oil, stirring constantly until meat is no longer pink. Remove meat from pan; set aside and keep warm.

Add a little more oil to the skillet and quickly sauté onions and celery until tender-crisp; add zucchini, thawed broccoli-cauliflower-carrot mix, and the chicken broth. Lower heat; cover and cook 2 or 3 minutes, until vegetables are tender-crisp. Add mushrooms.

Mix soy sauce, liquid from mushrooms, sugar, and cornstarch. Add cooked turkey to skillet. Stir in soy sauce mixture and mix gently to blend. Cook over low heat until sauce thickens a bit and clears. Cook 1 or 2 minutes more, adding a little more chicken broth if needed. Season to taste with lemon pepper or ginger if desired. Serve over fluffy rice. Serves 4 to 6.

Cook's Note: Using the frozen vegetable mix reduces preparation time by nearly half.

Turkey Tetrazini

1/4 cup onion, finely diced
2 Tablespoons margarine
1 3/4 Tablespoons flour
1/2 teaspoon salt (or to taste)
1/8 teaspoon pepper
1/4 teaspoon parsley flakes
1/2 cup chicken broth
1/2 cup milk
1/2 cup evaporated milk
1 can (4 ounces) sliced mush-
*   rooms, drained*
2 1/2 to 3 cups turkey, cooked
*   and diced*
6 to 7 ounces spaghetti, cooked
*   and drained*
1 cup shredded cheese (Monterey
*   Jack or mild Cheddar)*

Sauté onion in margarine until golden. Stir in flour, salt, pepper, and parsley flakes. Cook briefly then gradually add broth, stirring until mixture bubbles. Add milk, then evaporated milk in the same manner, stirring often to prevent sticking. When mixture comes to a boil, lower heat and simmer one minute. Stir in mushrooms.

In a large bowl, combine spaghetti and half of sauce, combining well. Add turkey and rest of sauce. Blend thoroughly.

Spoon mixture into a greased 9x13x2 baking dish. Sprinkle cheese over top. Bake at 350° F for 45 to 50 minutes or until hot throughout. Serves 8 to 10.

Cook's Note: This is the second-favorite casserole at Haus Edelweiss. Unchallenged first place goes to lasagna.

Perfect Gravy

2 1/2 cups rich broth from meat
(beef, pork, or turkey)
3/4 cup cold water
1/3 cup flour

Season broth as needed with instant beef or chicken bouillon (depending on the type of meat) and salt and pepper.

Place water and flour in a small jar with a tight lid. Shake well to blend. Remove the lid, allowing undissolved flour to fall back into the jar. Replace lid and shake again.

Heat broth to boiling; gradually add the flour and water mixture, stirring constantly. Bring back to a boil; lower heat and simmer for 2 to 3 minutes. Taste for seasoning. Makes 3 1/4 cups.

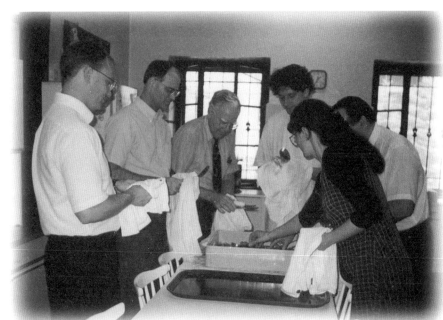

"Do Americans not like to eat potatoes?" a puz-
zled young first-time Polish student asked at
dinner one evening.
"Oh, yes," a short-term worker replied, "Ameri-
cans eat lots of potatoes."
But the uncertain look on the student's face
made it clear that, in his mind, potatoes
couldn't be very popular if they weren't
on the table every day!
Potatoes—cheap, filling, and readily avail-
able—are the basic staple throughout much of
Central and Eastern Europe. Potatoes are
boiled, baked, fried, or mashed; they are made
into porridge, pancakes, or dumplings. A failed
potato crop is disastrous in some areas for it sig-
nals a lean and hungry winter.
At Haus Edelweiss, we try to vary the menus by
serving pasta, potatoes, and rice. This explains
the Polish student's disbelief when pasta or rice
had been served for two days without
a sign of a potato.

Pasta
Potatoes
and Rice

A Haus of Prayer

All those who serve at Haus Edelweiss come to know that prayer is the very heart-beat of the Haus. Prayer sustains and furthers the work here and it provides the support and encouragement which undergirds every member of TCM's staff, both at Haus Edelweiss and at the international headquarters in Indianapolis, Indiana.

Supporters of this ministry form a small army of faithful prayer warriors who petition God daily on our behalf. What a blessing! To know that every day the halls of heaven are being flooded with prayers and petitions to support, maintain, and advance the work God is doing in Central and Eastern Europe.

In a special prayer ministry at the Haus, that loving embrace of prayer is extended to include our students and their families. The day after the students arrive for a conference, a prayer list containing the names of all attendees is distributed to the Americans. Each one is given the name(s) of one or more of our European guests to pray for; the Americans are asked to pray daily and specifically, throughout the conference, for the ones assigned to them. In addition, a card is provided on which a note of welcome and encouragement is printed, letting each one know that he or she is being lifted up in prayer every day. The cards are signed and placed on each beds the following morning by the Guest Services staff.

The sole purpose of this ministry of prayer is to lift up in love the needs and well being of our European brothers and sisters during the time they are studying at Haus Edelweiss; the more earnestly we pray for them, the more they become a part of us. God often uses prayer to change circumstances, but most often He uses it to change the pray-er.

Macaroni Supreme

12 ounces small shell macaroni

1 can cream of mushroom soup, undiluted

1 can (4 ounces) mushroom pieces, with juice

1 cup mayonnaise

1/4 teaspoon onion powder

1 pound shredded cheese (Cheddar or Monterey Jack)

3 Tablespoons margarine, melted

1/2 cup sesame seed or poppy seed snack crackers, crushed

Cook macaroni in boiling, salted water until just tender. Rinse and drain thoroughly. Combine mushroom soup, mushrooms and juice, mayonnaise, and onion powder, mixing well. Add macaroni and blend well. Spoon mixture into a greased 2 1/2-quart baking dish, or a 9x13x2 casserole.

Combine melted margarine and crumbs; sprinkle over the top. Bake at 375° F for about 35 minutes or until hot through. Serves 10.

Cook's Note: Years ago when I first came across this recipe, I used crushed Blue-cheese crackers for the topping. The flavor was a perfect match. Since these tasty little snacks are no longer available, I have tried several flavors. In Austria I use Vollkorn crackers, a rich wheat wafer—rather like a whole-wheat club cracker. Choose a rich, tasty cracker you like.

Noodles Romanoff

1/4 cup margarine
2 Tablespoons flour
1/2 teaspoon salt
1/4 teaspoon onion powder
1/16 teaspoon garlic powder
1 cup milk
1/2 cup sour cream
3/4 cup small curd cottage cheese
1/4 teaspoon paprika
1/4 cup grated Parmesan cheese
8 ounces medium noodles,
    cooked and drained
1/2 cup shredded cheese (mild
    Cheddar or Monterey Jack)

In a medium saucepan, melt margarine over medium heat. Stir in flour, salt, onion powder, and garlic powder to blend. Gradually add milk, stirring to prevent sticking. Cook until mixture comes to a boil; lower heat and cook until thickened (2 or 3 minutes). Cool slightly. Stir in sour cream, cottage cheese, paprika, and Parmesan cheese, blending well.

Place drained noodles in a large bowl; pour sauce over. Toss gently to completely coat noodles. Spoon into a greased 9x13 baking pan. Sprinkle with shredded cheese. Bake at 350° F for 1 hour or until hot and bubbly. Serves 8 to 10.

Cook's Note: A superb way to turn plain noodles into a company dish. Added to our file by a former cook.

Spaghetti and Cheese

*7 ounces spaghetti, cooked and
drained (do not rinse)*
*3 cups (12 ounces) shredded
Monterey Jack cheese*
2 eggs
2 1/2 cups milk
1 teaspoon salt (or to taste)
1/8 teaspoon pepper
1/2 teaspoon dry mustard
1 Tablespoon flour
2 Tablespoons margarine
paprika

In a greased 9x13x2 baking pan, place 1/3 of the spaghetti; sprinkle with 1/3 of the cheese. Repeat twice, making 3 layers.

In a small bowl, combine flour, dry mustard, salt, and pepper. Stir in about 1 Tablespoon of the milk to make a smooth paste. In another bowl, beat the eggs; blend in remaining milk and the flour mixture until smooth. Pour over spaghetti and cheese. Dot with margarine and dust lightly with paprika. Bake at 350° F for about 45 minutes or until set (the blade of a table knife inserted near the center should come out clean). Let stand several minutes before serving. Serves 8.

Cook's Note: For years this was my favorite "macaroni and cheese" recipe. Once I tried using spaghetti instead, the personality change was such a hit with my family that the name change became permanent. It has become popular also at Haus Edelweiss.

Au Gratin Potatoes

10 medium white potatoes
1 teaspoon salt
1/2 teaspoon pepper
1/2 teaspoon onion salt
2 cups (8 ounces) shredded
*   cheese (your choice)*
1 cup evaporated milk

Cook the potatoes in their jackets until tender. Drain well. CHILL several hours or overnight.

Peel potatoes; slice thin or shred coarsely. Combine seasonings. Layer potatoes and seasonings in a greased 9x13x2 baking dish. Sprinkle with cheese; pour evaporated milk over all. Bake at 350° F for 1 hour or until golden. Serves 12.

Cook's Note: Leftovers (if any) are a great addition to Potato Soup.

Oven Roasted Potatoes

8 medium baking potatoes,
*   unpeeled*
4 Tablespoons margarine, melted
4 teaspoons paprika
2 teaspoons salt
1 teaspoon pepper

Scrub potatoes and cut into large chunks. Place in a shallow, greased baking pan, allowing a little space between chunks. Drizzle with margarine. Combine seasonings and sprinkle over the potatoes. Bake uncovered at 375° F for 1 hour or until potatoes are tender. Serves 10.

Cook's Note: These quick, tasty potatoes are great with any kind of meat or poultry and are a hit with everyone.

Company Mashed Potatoes

5 pounds baking potatoes, peeled
*   and cut up*
1 package (8 ounces) cream
*   cheese, softened*
1 cup sour cream
1 teaspoon onion salt
1/2 teaspoon pepper
2 Tablespoons margarine, soft-
*   ened*
1/4 to 1/2 cup milk (as needed)

Cook potatoes in boiling salted water until tender. Drain well. Mash until smooth. Add the cream cheese (cut into small chunks), sour cream, seasonings, and margarine. Beat with an electric mixer until fluffy, adding milk a little at a time to desired consistency. Spoon potatoes into an oven-safe 2 1/2-quart dish or pan; cover. (Can be refrigerated up to a week.) To serve, bring potatoes to room temperature. Heat covered in a 325º F oven for 45 minutes or until piping hot. Serves 12.

Cook's Note: Smooth, creamy, and delicious, these potatoes are the perfect solution to mashed potatoes without the last-minute mess and clean-up. My eldest grandson, Michael, loves potatoes in any form but this is his very favorite. His wife Tammy shared this with us and we prepared Company Mashed Potatoes for Graduation Sunday dinner one year.

Parmesan Potato Sticks

6 medium baking potatoes
1/3 to 1/2 cup margarine, melted
1 cup Parmesan Coating
    (recipe follows)

Scrub potatoes; cut into 1/2 inch strips lengthwise then cut again to make strips 1/2" x 1/2." Drop into salted cold water to cover; let stand while you prepare the coating. Drain well and spread on towels to absorb water; pat with another towel to dry thoroughly.

Dip potato sticks in melted margarine; roll in Parmesan Coating. Place in a single layer, not touching, on baking sheets. Bake at 400° F for about 1 hour or until done and well browned. Serves 6 to 8.

Parmesan Coating

1/2 cup fine dry bread crumbs
1/2 cup grated Parmesan cheese
1/2 teaspoon salt
1/8 teaspoon pepper
1/8 teaspoon garlic powder
1/4 teaspoon paprika
1/2 teaspoon parsley flakes

Mix all ingredients together in a bowl.

Cook's Note: These are delicious. A great substitute for French Fries.

Potatoes Romanoff

6 medium baking potatoes
2 cups sour cream
1/2 teaspoon onion powder
1 1/2 teaspoons salt
1/2 teaspoon pepper
1 1/2 cups shredded cheese
paprika

Cook potatoes in their skins until tender. Cool completely before peeling. Shred potatoes into a large bowl. Combine sour cream and seasonings; add to the potatoes in the bowl along with the cheese. Mix well. Spoon into a greased 9x13x2 baking dish.

Cover and refrigerate 3 to 4 hours or overnight.

Bake at 350° F for 50 to 60 minutes, until hot through. Sprinkle lightly with paprika. Serves 8.

Cook's Note: Leftovers are a great addition to Potato Soup. Another delicious recipe from a former cook.

Ranch Potato Casserole

*6 to 8 medium potatoes (2 1/2
    to 3 pounds)*
1/2 cup sour cream
1/2 cup prepared ranch dressing
2 teaspoons parsley flakes
*1/4 cup bacon, cooked and
    crumbled (optional)*
*1 1/2 cups shredded cheese,
    DIVIDED*
2 cups crushed cornflakes
1/4 cup margarine, melted

Peel and quarter potatoes; cook until tender. Mix together the sour cream, ranch dressing, parsley flakes, bacon (if used), and 1 cup of the cheese. Add to potatoes and mix gently. Turn into a greased 9x13x2 baking dish. Sprinkle with remaining 1/2 cup cheese. Toss together the cornflake crumbs and melted margarine. Spread over top of cheese. Bake at 350° F for 40 to 45 minutes or until hot through. Serves 8.

Cook's Note: Ranch dressing mix is brought to Haus Edelweiss by short-term workers who know we cannot obtain it here. This tasty recipe was printed on one of the packages.

Twice-Baked Potatoes

8 large baking potatoes,
    scrubbed

1 1/3 cups sour cream

2/3 teaspoon onion powder

2/3 teaspoon salt

1/4 teaspoon pepper

8 ounces shredded cheddar cheese

1 cup milk

2 Tablespoons margarine, melted

Pierce potatoes several times with a fork or the tip of a paring knife. Bake at 400° F for 1 to 1 1/4 hours until tender. Let stand just a few minutes.

While potatoes are still hot, scoop out into a bowl, discarding the skins. Break up with a fork—DO NOT MASH. Add sour cream, seasonings, cheese, and milk, mixing lightly with a fork. Spoon into a greased 2-quart baking dish; drizzle with melted margarine and sprinkle with a little paprika. Bake at 375° F for 45 to 50 minutes until piping hot. Serves 8 to 10.

Cook's Note: This may be prepared ahead (even two or three days ahead) and refrigerated until needed. Remove from refrigerator an hour or more before baking. Increase baking time for cold casserole to 1 1/2 hours.

Easy Oven Rice

1 1/2 cups long-grain white rice
3/4 teaspoon salt
2 3/4 cups boiling water

Place all ingredients in a 2 1/2-quart baking dish. Cover tightly with foil. Bake at 350° F for 45 minutes, or until rice is tender and all liquid is absorbed. Uncover; fluff with a fork. Return to oven for 5 minutes. Serves 6 to 8.

Oven Rice Pilaf

1 1/2 cups long-grain white rice
3 Tablespoons golden raisins
1 Tablespoon instant chicken
    bouillon
1/8 teaspoon onion powder
1/3 cup celery, diced fine
1/2 teaspoon salt
2 Tablespoons margarine
2 1/2 cups boiling water

In a 1 1/2 to 2-quart casserole combine the rice, raisins, instant bouillon, onion powder, celery, salt, and margarine. Pour the boiling water over all; stir to combine. Cover tightly with foil. Bake at 350° F for 1 hour. Uncover; fluff rice with a fork. Bake uncovered another 5 minutes. Serves 6 to 8.

Yankee Fried Rice

1/4 cup margarine
1/2 cup diced onion
1 1/2 cups long-grain white rice
2 3/4 cups water
1 chicken bouillon cube
1/2 teaspoon salt
1/8 teaspoon pepper

In a heavy, medium-sized saucepan, over medium heat, sauté onion in margarine until transparent. Add the rice and cook, stirring constantly until rice is a rich, deep golden brown. Lower heat as needed to prevent burning. Remove from heat and pour water in SLOWLY to prevent a rush of hot steam. Add seasonings and stir. Bring to a boil; reduce heat to very low; cover and simmer about 20 minutes until rice is tender and all moisture is absorbed. Fluff with a fork; taste for seasoning. Serves 8 to 10.

Cook's Note: At Haus Edelweiss, this is everyone's favorite way to enjoy rice.

Haus Edelweiss Prayer

*Have I not commanded You? Be strong and courageous. Do
not be terrified; do not be discouraged, for the Lord your
God will be with you wherever you go.*

*Anyone who serves Christ in this way is pleasing to God and
approved by men.*

*Unless the Lord builds the house [Haus], its builders labor in
vain.*

Set your minds on things above, not on earthly things.

Encourage one another . . .

Devote yourselves to prayer . . .

*Evening and morning, and at noon will I pray and cry aloud;
and He will hear my voice.*

*Let your light so shine before men that they may see your good
works and glorify your father which is in heaven.*

*Whatever you do, work at it with all your heart as working for
the Lord and not for men.*

*Enter his gates with thanksgiving, and his courts with praise;
Give thanks to him, bless his name.*

*I pray that out of his glorious riches he may strengthen you
with power through his spirit in your inner being.*

*Seek ye first the kingdom of God and his righteousness, and all
these things shall be added unto you*

*Since you know you will receive an inheritance from the Lord
as a reward, it is the Lord Christ you are serving.*

*Joshua 1:9, Romans 14:18, Psalm 127:1, Colossians 3:2,
Hebrews 10:25 (RSV), Colossians 4:2, Psalm 55:17 (KJV),
Matthew 5:16 (KJV), Colossians 3:23, Psalm 100:4,
Ephesians 3:16, Matthew 6:33 (KJV), Colossians 3:24*

*Compiled by and used with permission from Sharon Howells from
Valley Christian Church in Rosemount, Minnesota.*

Swimming in an outdoor pool (even a heated one) when the air temperature is 42 degrees Fahrenheit would tempt only the hardiest "Polar Bear Club" types in America. Not so our Estonian students. When one is accustomed to swimming in the frigid water of the Baltic Sea—what's the problem??? Steam rising from the surface of the pool may be so thick it looks like fog on late September mornings, but every morning between 7:00 and 7:30 half a dozen or so Estonians swim before breakfast.

The tiled pool (donated more than twenty years ago by a former TCM board member) is located between the Big Haus and the Leadership Training Center. Americans, viewing the scene from the snug warmth of the kitchen, rub their arms and shiver, muttering, "Just THINKING about that makes me cold!"

International
Foods

Die Jause

A very special Austrian tradition, rather like the British high tea, is the Jause (pronounced YOW-zuh). It is served in the later afternoon to early evening. Sweets, pastries, savories, and small snacks are served along with beverages. Sweets are served first. (My kind of party!)

At Haus Edelweiss a Jause has been used to entertain our Austrian colleagues at a time prior to the opening of the conference season. It is a very festive dress-up occasion with the women often dressed in "Trachten mode" (native or regional fashion).

The first course—a wonderful array of sweet treats—is served with guests seated around a table beautifully set with the best china, linen, silver, and fresh flowers. Coffee and tea are offered with this course. In the Austrian fashion, the strong coffee is served in small cups with sugar and unsweetened whipped cream, a treat called Kaffee Melange. This is a relaxed, leisurely time, an opportunity to chat and visit and enjoy the company of friends as the plates of sweets are passed. After a time the table is cleared and guests move to more comfortable seating. Plates and trays of small savories and finger foods are set out on a coffee table or other surface convenient to the seating area. Beverages such as a sparkling water and apple juice are offered. "Apfelsaft Gespritzt," made of equal parts apple juice and sparkling mineral water, is a refreshing, popular choice.

For the sweet course it is common to offer three or four desserts. A beautifully frosted cake such as Coronation Cake or Chocolate Tweed Cake may be the main feature. Accompanying this will be one or two plates of dainty cookies such as Mexican Wedding Cakes, Lemon Bars cut into 1-inch squares, Macaroons, or a small tray of tiny tarts. A pretty glass plate of assorted fresh fruit—halved orange slices, thin slices of crisp apple, whole strawberries (with cap attached), kiwi slices, seedless grapes, or Nutty Bananas for example—offers a pleasant contrast. (Note that "small" and "tiny" are adjectives frequently used here. Portions are indeed small but plates of pastries are passed frequently during this unhurried time.)

A wide array of savories is available. Popular choices are finger sandwiches, using a variety of breads (though not sweet breads), and creamy fillings such as egg salad, tuna salad, or a cream cheese spread. Deviled eggs, salami, or ham "stacks" using cream cheese to layer slices of meat (cut into small triangles) are other choices. Hot bite-size hors d'oeuvres are also good. Again, three choices are usually offered along with small bowls of stuffed green olives, mixed nuts, and/or miniature pretzels.

Perhaps you will be inspired to try the "Austrian way" for your next special occasion party and surprise your friends by providing a "cross-cultural experience" right in your own home.

Recipes for Coronation Cake and Chocolate Tweed Cake are in the Desserts section. Baked Do-Nut Holes are included in the Breads section. Mexican Wedding Cake and Lemon Bars can be found in the Cookies, Bars, and Brownies section. Nutty Bananas appears in the Salad section.

AUSTRIA

Wiener Schnitzel

(Breaded Cutlet)

4 pork cutlets, pounded thin
(1/8 to 1/4 inch)
salt and pepper
1/2 cup milk
1/2 cup flour
2 eggs, beaten
1/2 cup fine bread crumbs
oil for frying

Rinse the meat and pat dry with paper towels, sprinkle with salt and pepper. Moisten with milk, dredge in flour, then dredge in egg, then dredge in bread crumbs, making sure that it is well coated at each step. Cook in a deep fryer or fry in a skillet in at least 1/4 inch of hot oil until golden brown; serve with lemon wedges.

Cook's Note: The word "Wiener" (pronounced VEE-nr) comes from Wien, the German name for Austria's capital, Vienna. Wiener Schnitzel can be found on virtually every restaurant menu in Austria, and is also common in restaurants in the surrounding countries (Czech Republic, Slovakia, Hungary, northern Italy) that were part of the Austro-Hungarian empire.

Haus Hint: Boneless, skinless chicken or turkey breast can also be "schnitzeled." The breasts should be butterflied by cutting them almost all the way through the middle horizontally with a sharp knife, then laid open to make one flat piece. If you want a thinner poultry schnitzel, put the pieces one at a time in a plastic bag and roll firmly with a rolling pin to the desired thickness. DO NOT pound poultry or it will turn into a gelatinous goo. Dry, dredge, and fry as for pork schnitzels.

CZECH REPUBLIC

Dusene' Zeli

(Czech Cabbage)

*1/2 cup (1 medium) onion,
    finely diced*
2 to 3 teaspoons oil
*2 cups (500 grams) packaged
    sauerkraut (the type found in
    the dairy case)*
water
*1/2 to 1 teaspoon crushed caraway
    seed, to taste*
1 to 2 Tablespoons sugar
1 medium potato, finely grated
salt to taste

In a medium skillet, sauté the onion in a little oil until it begins to brown. Rinse sauerkraut thoroughly in cold water and drain. Add to onion in skillet with just enough water to cover; sprinkle with caraway seeds. Cover and simmer until cabbage (sauerkraut) begins to get soft, about 10 to 15 minutes. Add 1 Tablespoon sugar and additional water as needed. Continue cooking another 10 to 15 minutes. Fold in the grated potato and continue folding as cabbage thickens. Add salt, if needed, to taste, and more sugar if desired. Serves 3 to 4.

Cook's Note: Cabbage and potatoes are dietary mainstays throughout Central and Eastern Europe. This traditional side dish was shared by the wife of TCM's Field Director for Czech Republic.

ESTONIA

Keedetud Soolakala Kartulitega

(Boiled Fish and Potatoes)

8 to 10 potatoes, peeled
3 cups water
salt
2 pounds fish (pike, perch, or
*   flounder)*
2 Tablespoons butter
1 small onion, chopped
1 to 2 Tablespoons flour

Put the potatoes in hot salted water and bring to a boil. Lower heat and simmer until almost tender. Cover the potatoes with the whole cleaned fish (or fish pieces) and cook until tender. Lift the fish and potatoes gently onto a serving dish or platter. Strain the stock and set aside. Sauté the onion in butter; stir in the flour until smooth. Add the strained stock and cook until sauce thickens and boils. Season to taste with salt and pepper. Serve sauce with the fish and potatoes. Serves 4 to 6.

Cook's Note: Fish, fresh or salted, is a fundamental part of the Estonian diet. Estonia is located on the Baltic Sea, up near the top of the map of Europe, separated from Finland by only a narrow strip of ocean. This recipe came from the cookbook Estonian Cuisine which was given to us by TCM's Field Director for the Baltic Republics (Estonia, Latvia, and Lithuania).

HUNGARY

Csirke Paprikas

(Chicken Paprika)

1 1/2 to 2 medium onions,
    chopped
3 Tablespoons oil
3 to 4 Tablespoons HUNGARIAN
    paprika, divided
1/2 to 1 teaspoon salt (to taste)
1 whole chicken, cut up or 2 to
    2 1/2 pounds of chicken pieces
    WITH SKIN and bones
1 tomato, quartered
1 green pepper, quartered
2 Tablespoons sour cream

In a large covered pot, sauté onions in oil over low heat until onions begin to clear. Mix in 2 Tablespoons paprika and salt. Add chicken pieces. Cover and continue to cook over low heat until the skin begins to pull away from the chicken (about 30 to 40 minutes). Turn chicken once or twice and stir occasionally, but keep dish covered as much as possible. When the skins begin to pull away from the chicken add the tomato, green pepper, and 1 to 2 Tablespoons paprika (the mixture should have a rich paprika color). Cover and continue cooking until chicken is completely cooked (10 to 15 minutes). Remove chicken pieces and green pepper from the pot. Pour the remaining mixture into a blender. Peel the skins off the chicken pieces and add to the mixture in the blender, along with 1 or 2 pieces of green pepper. Blend mixture into a sauce. Blend in the sour cream. Serve the chicken and sauce with rice. The moisture created while cooking determines this recipe's success. It is very important to keep the lid on the pot while cooking.

Cook's Note: Hungary has a wide and varied cuisine, making it difficult to select just one recipe. The wife of TCM's Field Director for Hungary gave us a book of recipes from which to choose. The recipe here is the favorite dish of Joska Temesvary, staff member at Haus Edelweiss. (Joska's parents emigrated from Hungary to the United States in the 1920s.)

POLAND

Knedle

(Dumpling with Plums)

1 1/2 pounds potatoes
1 Tablespoon sour cream
1 Tablespoon butter
1 egg
salt
1 3/4 cups flour
1 2/3 pounds small plums
1/2 cup icing sugar
2 Tablespoons cinnamon
4 Tablespoons butter, melted
3 Tablespoons bread crumbs

Wash and peel potatoes. Cook in salted water, drain, cool, and mince. Add sour cream, butter, egg, salt, and enough flour to knead the dough.

Wash the plums, pat dry and remove stone (without cutting completely through the plum). Stuff each plum with sugar mixed with cinnamon.

Roll out the dough into 1/8 inch thick sheet and cut into approximately 3x3 inch squares. Place one plum on each square, seal and shape into dumpling. Cook a few at a time in boiling salted water until they emerge on the surface. Take the dumpling out with a slotted spoon.

Melt butter in a frying pan, add bread crumbs and lightly fry. Add the dumplings, mix well, turning on all sides. Transfer to a serving plate, sprinkle with icing sugar mixed with cinnamon and serve.

*Cook's Note: This recipe came from the cookbook **Polish Cooking** which was given to us by TCM's Field Director for Poland.*

ROMANIA

Rice Pudding

6 Tablespoons rice
4 cups milk
1/2 cup cream
1/2 teaspoon salt
1 Tablespoon sugar
2 Tablespoons raisins

In the top of a double boiler combine rice and milk. Mix in cream, salt, and sugar. Cover and cook over low heat 2 1/2 to 3 hours, until rice is soft.

Cook's Note: This recipe has been in the TCM files for so long, I'm not sure who gave it to us originally. But I know it's a tasty and easy dessert for almost any meal.

RUSSIA

Golubtsi

(Lazy Cabbage)

2 pounds cabbage
1 pound ground beef
3/4 cup rice
6 or 7 tomatoes, cut
2 onions, diced
2 to 3 Tablespoons butter
salt
2 cups sour cream

Cut the cabbage into pieces (1/2 inch square). Rinse the rice. Cut tomatoes and onions. Grease a pan with butter and put in the following ingredients by layers in this order: tomatoes, rice, meat, onions, cabbage, and so on until all the ingredients are used. Salt every layer a little. Pour sour cream over everything and put the pan on the stove (small heat). Cook until ready, stirring from time to time.

Cook's Note: This simple meal-in-a-dish is a family favorite prepared by the wife of TCM's Field Director for Russia.

UKRAINE

Borshch

(Beet Soup)

5 to 6 cups water
1 pound beef on the bone
1 pound potatoes (about 3 medi-
um), peeled and cut up
1 pound white cabbage
1/2 pound fresh red beets
1/2 Tablespoon vinegar
1 teaspoon sugar
1 Tablespoon fat (from beef
broth)
salt (to taste)
3/4 cup tomato paste
1 carrot, julienned
1 onion, julienned
1 parsley root (or leaves to taste)
1 teaspoon flour
1 bay leaf
2 Tablespoons butter
1 clove garlic, pressed
2 pepper corns
hot red pepper (optional)
1 sweet green pepper, sliced
2 or 3 fresh tomatoes, sliced
3/4 cup sour cream
fresh parsley or dill to garnish

Make a broth of the beef on the bone. When the meat is soft, remove and cut into chunks. (Skim some of the fat from the broth to use later.) Salt the broth; add potatoes and boil until half-cooked (10 to 15 minutes). Using a very sharp knife, cut cabbage and beets in long, VERY THIN shreds—like thin straws. In another pan, cook beets: sprinkle with vinegar, add salt, fat of the meat which boiled in the broth, tomato paste, and sugar. Steam until it is almost tender. Add beet mixture and cabbage to the broth when potatoes are half-cooked. Be careful not to overcook the cabbage; it quickly becomes soft.

In another pan, sauté onion in butter. Add carrots and parsley, and steam until tender. Add flour and mix until smooth. Add onion mixture to broth with bay leaf and peppercorns. If desired, add a little hot red pepper. When the vegetables are soft enough, add the garlic and boil for 3 minutes. Remove from heat for 30 minutes to 3 hours. Remove parsley root, bay leaf, and peppercorns. Add sweet pepper and fresh tomatoes, and bring to a boil for 1 to 5 minutes. Then leave them in or take out, as you please. Serve in soup plates with a chunk of meat and some sour cream; garnish with fresh parsley or dill. Serve with garlic bread.

Cook's Note: Borsch is a basic staple of the Ukrainian diet and there are as many recipes for it as there are cooks who make it. This one was given to us by one of our Master of Arts students from Ukraine.

"Thank you for the refreshment in spirit and body during the two weeks here. Your love and joyful working are an example for us to follow. We don't stop praying for you."

The Hungarian Delegation

Cookies
Bars
and Brownies

Love and Laughter

The languages of Central and Eastern Europe do not roll easily off most American tongues. We wonder how in the world we could possibly pronounce all those consonants! Conquering a simple "Hello" or "Good morning" in Hungarian (Joreggelt)*, or Polish (Dzien dobry)* is usually difficult for newcomers. Even some staff members who have been around for many conferences often admit that "Good morning" exhausts their entire vocabulary. A few revert to "Grüss Gott" (a typical Austrian greeting meaning "May God greet you") just to help them feel a part of the international mix. But love and laughter are universal languages. Ethnic differences and national borders become unimportant, and communication is heart to heart, friend to friend.

Brave American souls are often challenged, however, by the desire to understand what the persons sitting near them at the table are saying and an equally compelling need to be understood. So with the help of a "crib sheet" listing some of the common words and phrases in the language of the visiting group(s), along with corresponding English words, they make a stab at it.

For the first few days the Europeans smile and nod encouragingly as they politely try to correct pronunciation. By the end of the week, people have had a chance to become better acquainted and everyone is more relaxed in this cross-cultural setting. In fact, the tables often erupt in gales of laughter as mispronounced words fill the air.

One such episode occurred a few years ago when the visiting group was from Hungary. Once the laughter had subsided a bit, one of the Hungarian translators called out, "It is O.K. In heaven we will all speak Hungarian—because it takes an eternity to learn!" But another Hungarian preacher pointed out that "Hungarian can't be that difficult; our little children can speak it!"

*Pronunciations: yo-ra-GELT, jen DO-bree.

Almond Cookies

2 3/4 cups flour
1 cup sugar
1/2 teaspoon baking soda
1/2 teaspoon salt
1 cup butter or margarine
1 egg, slightly beaten
1 teaspoon almond extract
1/3 cup whole almonds

In a bowl, stir together flour, sugar, baking soda, and salt. Cut in butter to form a meal-like texture. Add the egg and almond extract; mix well.

Shape dough into 1-inch balls. Place 2 inches apart on ungreased (or parchment paper-lined) baking sheets. Press an almond onto the top of each cookie, flattening slightly. Bake at 325º F for about 15 minutes. Cool on racks. Makes 4 1/2 dozen.

Cook's Note: In an average year, more than 8,000 cookies are baked in the Haus Edelweiss kitchen. Cookies are served as lunch dessert four or five times during each conference. Since 14 to 15 dozen are needed for just one meal, we normally prepare enough dough for 14 to 20 dozen of each kind. Even with those quantities, we can't keep the cookie tin full of homemade cookies for snacks.

Butterscotch Crisps

1 cup sugar
2 cups light brown sugar, packed
1 1/2 cups margarine, softened
3 eggs
1 1/2 teaspoons vanilla
3 1/4 cups flour
3/4 teaspoon salt
2 1/4 teaspoons baking soda
1 1/2 cups lightly crushed
    cornflakes

Thoroughly cream the sugar, brown sugar, and margarine. Beat in eggs and vanilla. In a separate bowl, stir together the flour, salt, and baking soda. Gradually mix dry ingredients into creamed mixture. Stir in cornflakes.

Cover and CHILL DOUGH several hours or overnight.

Shape into 1-inch balls (or use a level #40 scoop). Place at least 2 inches apart on ungreased (or parchment paper-lined) baking sheets. Bake at 375° F for 12 to 15 minutes. (After "puffing" up just a little, cookies should look flattened out.) Cool on baking sheet 1 minute before removing to racks to cool completely. Makes 4 1/2 dozen 3-inch cookies.

Cook's Note: A crisp-but-chewy cookie, similar to the Potato Chip Cookies but with a much lower fat content.

Chewy Chocolate Cookies

2 cups sugar
1 1/4 cups margarine, softened
2 eggs
2 teaspoons vanilla
2 cups flour
3/4 cup cocoa
1 teaspoon baking soda
dash of salt
1 cup chopped nuts (optional)

Thoroughly cream the sugar and margarine until fluffy. Beat in eggs and vanilla. In a separate bowl, combine flour, cocoa, baking soda, and salt. Gradually stir into the creamed mixture, blending completely. Mix in nuts if used.

Drop by teaspoonfuls onto ungreased (or parchment paper-lined) baking sheets. Bake at 350° F for 8 to 9 minutes. DO NOT OVERBAKE! Cookies will be soft. Cool on baking sheet 1 minute before removing to racks to cool completely. Makes 4 to 4 1/2 dozen.

*Cook's Note: A delight for the true chocoholic. This recipe came from a **Taste of Country** cookbook. Really yummy!*

*Recipe reprinted with permission from **Taste of Country** Cookbook, Reiman Publishing*

Chocolate Oatmeal Cookies

1 1/2 cups sugar
1 cup light brown sugar, packed
1 cup margarine, softened
2 eggs
2 teaspoons vanilla
1 1/2 cups flour
1/2 cup cocoa
1 teaspoon baking soda
1/2 teaspoon salt
3 cups oatmeal

Cream together the sugar, brown sugar, and margarine until light and fluffy. Beat in the eggs and vanilla until well mixed.

In a separate bowl, stir together the flour, cocoa, baking soda, and salt. Add gradually to creamed mixture; blend well. Blend in the oatmeal. Dough will be stiff.

Shape into 1-inch balls (or use a level #40 scoop); drop about 2 inches apart on ungreased (or parchment paper-lined) baking sheets. Bake at 350° F for about 12 minutes or just until set but still a bit moist in the center. DO NOT OVER-BAKE. Cool on baking sheet 1 minute before removing to racks to cool completely. Makes 3 1/2 to 4 dozen.

Cook's Note: These delicious cookies are a little chewy with an intensely chocolate flavor. The inspired contribution of an earlier cook.

Cowboy Cookies

1 cup sugar

1 cup light brown sugar, packed

1 cup margarine or shortening,
    softened

2 large eggs

1 teaspoon vanilla

2 cups flour

1 teaspoon baking soda

1/2 teaspoon salt

1/2 teaspoon baking powder

2 cups oatmeal

1 1/3 cups (8 ounces) chocolate
    chips

Cream together thoroughly the sugar, brown sugar, and margarine. Add eggs and vanilla, beating until fluffy and well blended.

In a separate bowl, stir together the flour, baking soda, salt, and baking powder. Gradually stir into creamed mixture to blend well. Stir in oatmeal and chocolate chips, mixing completely.

Shape into 1 1/4-inch balls (or use a #40 scoop); place 2 inches apart on lightly greased (or parchment paper-lined) baking sheets. Bake at 375º F for 12 to 15 minutes. Cool on racks. Makes 4 1/2 dozen.

Ginger Snaps

1 cup sugar
3/4 cup shortening
1 egg
1/4 cup molasses (mild, not
  blackstrap)
2 cups flour
1 Tablespoon ginger
2 teaspoons baking soda
1/2 teaspoon salt
1 teaspoon cinnamon
additional sugar for rolling

Cream together well the sugar and shortening; beat in egg and molasses. In a separate bowl, stir together flour, ginger, baking soda, salt, and cinnamon. Gradually blend dry ingredients into creamed mixture.

Shape into 1-inch balls (or slightly smaller if desired); roll in additional sugar. Place 2 inches apart on lightly greased (or parchment paper-lined) baking sheets. Bake at 375° F for about 10 minutes. (Cookies will puff up, then flatten out with crinkly tops.) Cool on racks. Makes 4 dozen small cookies.

Cook's Note: A friend in Washington Township Homemaker's Club in Indiana shared this recipe. A number of years ago I entered the cookies in the Indiana State Fair where they took a blue ribbon.

Grandma's Sugar Cookies

1 1/2 cups sugar
1 1/3 cups margarine, softened
2 eggs
2 teaspoons vanilla
3 1/2 cups flour
2 teaspoons baking powder
pinch of salt
additional sugar for coating

Cream together the sugar and margarine. Add eggs and vanilla; beat well. In a separate bowl, combine the flour, baking powder, and salt. Add dry ingredients gradually to creamed mixture, working in the last cup of flour with your hands. Shape into a roll 2 to 2 1/2 inches in diameter. Wrap in plastic wrap or waxed paper. CHILL OVERNIGHT or freeze. (If frozen, thaw only slightly before slicing.)

Slice 1/8 inch thick, using a sharp, thin-bladed knife. Dip the top of each slice in sugar and place on ungreased (or parchment paper-lined) baking sheets. Bake at 375º F for about 12 to 15 minutes. Cool on racks. Makes 4 1/2 to 5 dozen.

Cook's Note: These old-fashioned Sugar Cookies are SO versatile! If you prefer, the dough can be rolled out on a lightly floured surface and cut with cookie cutters into desired shapes. Sprinkle tops with colored sugar. Or try dipping the slices in a sugar-cinnamon mixture—use a ratio of 2 teaspoons cinnamon to 2 Tablespoons sugar.

This recipe was shared by my niece, Janice Miller, who remembers her grandmother making them.

Molasses Cookies

1 1/2 cups shortening, melted
   and cooled
2 cups sugar
1/2 cup molasses (mild)
2 eggs
4 cups flour
4 teaspoons baking soda
2 teaspoons cloves
2 teaspoons cinnamon
1 teaspoon salt
1 teaspoon ginger
additional sugar for rolling

Beat together the melted shortening, sugar, molasses, and eggs. In a separate bowl, stir together flour, baking soda, cloves, cinnamon, salt, and ginger. Gradually stir dry ingredients into the molasses mixture, blending well.

Shape into 1 1/4-inch balls (or use a level #40 scoop). Roll in additional sugar. Place 2 or more inches apart on lightly greased (or parchment paper-lined) baking sheets. Bake at 350° F for 15 minutes until set but still soft in the center. Cool on baking sheet 1 minute before removing to racks to cool completely. Makes 3 1/2 dozen 3-inch cookies.

Cook's Note: Old-fashioned flavor and a slightly chewy texture. These are the favorite cookies of one of our professors. We always try to serve them when he is here.

Since molasses is also on the "unavailable" list in Austria, we rely on our faithful short-term workers from the U.S. to replenish our supply when they come to the Haus.

Oatmeal Raisin Cookies

1/2 cup sugar
1 cup brown sugar, packed
3/4 cup margarine, softened
2 eggs
2 Tablespoons milk (or water)
1/2 teaspoon vanilla
1 1/2 cups flour
1 teaspoon salt
1 teaspoon baking soda
1 1/2 teaspoons cinnamon
3 cups oatmeal
1 cup raisins
3/4 cup chopped walnuts
   (optional)

Thoroughly cream together sugar, brown sugar, and margarine. Add eggs, milk, and vanilla; beat well. In a separate bowl, mix together flour, salt, baking soda, and cinnamon. Add dry ingredients gradually to creamed mixture, blending well. Add oatmeal, raisins (and nuts if used). Mix very thoroughly.

Drop by rounded teaspoons (or use a level #40 scoop) onto greased (or parchment paper-lined) baking sheets. Bake at 350° F for 12 to 15 minutes, until very lightly browned. Cool on racks. Makes 3 1/2 dozen.

(The Best!) Peanut Butter Cookies

2 cups sugar
2 cups light brown sugar, packed
2 cups margarine, softened
2 cups shortening
2 cups creamy-style
     peanut butter
4 eggs
5 1/2 cups flour
3 teaspoons baking soda
1 teaspoon salt
2 teaspoons baking powder

Cream together very thoroughly the sugar, brown sugar, margarine, shortening, and peanut butter. Add eggs and beat until well blended. In a separate bowl, combine the flour, baking soda, salt, and baking powder. Gradually add dry ingredients to creamed mixture, mixing thoroughly.

Shape into 1 1/4 inch balls (or use a level #40 scoop); place 2 to 3 inches apart on ungreased (or parchment paper-lined) baking sheets. (No need to flatten.) Bake at 375º F until set but not brown—about 12 to 15 minutes. (Cookies will be light brown on the bottom.) DO NOT OVERBAKE. Cool on baking sheet 1 minute before removing to racks to cool completely. Makes 8 dozen 3-inch cookies.

Cook's Note: By popular vote, THE BEST Peanut Butter Cookies. At Haus Edelweiss, we make double this amount for each conference.

*The recipe came from my long-ago **Better Homes and Gardens Cook Book**, and though I have tried MANY others over the years, not one has measured up to this one. They freeze well, too, packed in an airtight rigid container. This recipe is copyrighted material of Meredith Corporation, used with their permission. All rights reserved.*

Jo's Peanutty Chocolate Chip Cookies

1/2 cup sugar
1/2 cup light brown sugar, packed
1/2 cup margarine, softened
1/2 cup chunky peanut butter
1 egg
1 3/8 cups flour
3/4 teaspoon baking soda
1/2 teaspoon baking powder
1/4 teaspoon salt
3/4 cup semi-sweet chocolate chips

Cream together the sugar, brown sugar, margarine, and peanut butter until light and fluffy. Add the egg and beat well. In a separate bowl combine flour, baking soda, baking powder, and salt. Add gradually to creamed mixture, blending completely. Mix in the chocolate chips.

Drop by rounded teaspoons onto ungreased (or parchment paper-lined) baking sheets. Bake at 375º F for 8 to 10 minutes or until set and light brown on the bottom. Don't over bake. Cool on racks. Makes 4 dozen.

Cook's Note: Cookie dough is usually prepared well in advance, during the times prior to conference, and stored in the freezer. Using a #40 scoop, dough is dropped onto baking sheets—close together but not touching—and frozen for two hours or more. Frozen balls of cookie dough are then transferred to heavy duty plastic bags (7 to 9 dozen per bag) and returned to the freezer. When ready to use, the frozen dough can be arranged on baking sheets to thaw before baking.

Potato Chip Cookies

1 1/2 cups sugar

1 1/2 cups light brown sugar, packed

1 1/2 cups shortening

3 eggs

1 1/2 teaspoons vanilla

3 1/4 cups flour

3/4 teaspoon salt

2 1/4 teaspoons baking soda

1 1/2 cups crushed potato chips

Thoroughly cream the sugar, brown sugar, and shortening until fluffy. Add eggs and vanilla and beat well. In a separate bowl, stir together the flour, salt, and baking soda. Gradually stir into creamed mixture until completely blended. Blend in potato chips. CHILL DOUGH 1 hour.

Shape into 1-inch balls (or use a level #40 scoop). Place 3 inches apart on ungreased (or parchment paper-lined) baking sheets. Don't crowd—they spread! Bake at 375° F for 12 to 15 minutes, or until a rich golden brown. Cool on racks. Makes about 4 dozen.

Cook's Note: Although the "Cookies" section is the largest one in my personal recipe box, I had never heard of Potato Chip Cookies until my first visit to Haus Edelweiss. Former cook Lois Powney says she made these using the crumbs in the bottom of the potato chip bag when her children were growing up. Crisp and chewy, they have become a tradition at the Haus.

Snickerdoodles

2 1/4 cups sugar
1 1/2 cups margarine, melted
3 eggs
4 cups + 2 Tablespoons flour
1 Tablespoon cream of tartar
1 1/2 teaspoons baking soda
3/8 teaspoon salt
4 Tablespoons sugar (for rolling)
1 Tablespoon cinnamon (for
  rolling)

Thoroughly cream the margarine and sugar; add eggs and beat well. In a separate bowl, combine the flour, cream of tartar, baking soda, and salt. Gradually stir into the creamed mixture.

Stir together the sugar and cinnamon in a shallow bowl.

Shape dough into 1-inch balls (or use a level #40 scoop). Roll in cinnamon-sugar mixture. Place 2 inches apart on ungreased (or parchment paper-lined) baking sheets. Bake at 400° F for about 12 to 15 minutes, until light brown. Cookies will puff up then flatten out with crinkly tops. Cool on racks. Makes about 4 dozen.

Cook's Note: A favorite after-school treat when my boys were growing up: Snickerdoodles, warm from the oven, and a big glass of cold milk. When the staff at Haus Edelweiss voted for their personal favorites, Julia Simmons, our Guest Services Coordinator, chose Snickerdoodles.

Almond Spice Bars

1 box Spice cake mix
2 Tablespoons sugar
2 eggs
1/2 cup margarine, melted
1 1/4 cups water
1/2 cup chopped almonds
Orange Glaze (recipe below)

Combine all ingredients except almonds in a large mixing bowl. Beat to blend well. Stir in almonds. Pour into a greased 15x10x1 pan. Bake at 375° F for 20 to 25 minutes or until it tests done (a wooden pick inserted in center comes out clean). Cool slightly. Drizzle with Orange Glaze. Cool. Cut into bars of desired size.

Orange Glaze: Blend together 1 1/2 cups sifted powdered sugar and enough orange juice to make a pourable consistency (about 2 or 3 Tablespoons).

Cook's Note: Super easy. Carrot cake mix with chopped walnuts is equally good.

Banana Orange Bars

1 2/3 cups sugar
1 cup oil
4 eggs
2 cups mashed ripe bananas
2 cups flour
2 teaspoons baking powder
1 teaspoon baking soda
2 teaspoons cinnamon
1 teaspoon salt
Orange Butter Frosting (recipe
   below)

In a large mixing bowl beat together sugar, oil, eggs, and bananas. In a separate bowl, stir together flour, baking powder, baking soda, cinnamon, and salt. Gradually add dry ingredients to creamed mixture, folding in until completely blended. Pour mixture into a greased 15x10x1 pan. Bake at 350º F for about 25 to 30 minutes, until it tests done (a wooden pick inserted in center comes out clean). Cool completely. Frost with Orange Butter Frosting. Makes 24 to 36 bars.

Orange Butter Frosting

3 cups sifted powdered sugar
1/4 cup margarine, softened
1/4 cup orange juice
1/2 teaspoon grated orange peel

Beat all ingredients together in a small mixing bowl until smooth. Spread over cooled bars.

Cook's Note: Another delicious treat from **Taste of Country**. _A big dessert hit at the Haus._

Recipe reprinted with permission from **Taste of Country Cookbook**, _Reiman Publishing_

"Chocodile" Bars

1 1/4 cups light brown sugar,
    packed
1 cup margarine, softened
1/3 cup crunchy peanut butter
1 egg
1 teaspoon vanilla
1/2 teaspoon salt
2 1/2 cups flour
Topping (recipe below)

Cream together the brown sugar, margarine, and peanut butter. Beat in egg and vanilla. Gradually mix in salt and flour. Press evenly into an ungreased 15x10x1 baking pan. Bake at 350º F for 20 to 25 minutes until golden. Cool slightly. Spread with Topping. Cool before cutting. Makes 24 to 36 bars.

Topping

1 cup semi-sweet chocolate chips
1/2 cup peanut butter (regular
    or chunky)
1 1/2 cups cornflakes

In a medium saucepan melt the chocolate chips and peanut butter; stir in cornflakes to coat well. Spread on the still-warm bars.

Fruit Cocktail Bars

2 eggs
1 1/2 cups sugar
2 cups undrained fruit cocktail
1 teaspoon vanilla
2 1/4 cups flour
1 1/2 teaspoons baking soda
1 teaspoon salt
1 1/3 cups flaked coconut
1/2 cup chopped walnuts
Glaze (recipe below)

Beat together the eggs and sugar; add undrained fruit cocktail and vanilla and mix well. In a separate bowl, combine the flour, baking soda, and salt; stir into fruit mixture and blend well. Spread in a greased 15x10x1 pan. Sprinkle coconut and nuts evenly over the top. Bake at 350° F for 20 to 25 minutes or until it tests done (a wooden pick inserted in center comes out clean). Cool 10 minutes; drizzle with Glaze. Cool completely before cutting. Makes 24 bars (2 1/2 x 2 1/2 inches square).

Glaze

1/2 cup sugar
1/4 cup margarine
2 Tablespoons milk
1/4 teaspoon vanilla

Combine sugar, margarine, and milk in a small saucepan. Bring to a boil over low heat. Remove from heat; stir in vanilla.

Cook's Note: At Haus Edelweiss we cut this into large pieces (about 15 per pan) and serve with whipped topping for dinner dessert. (The Austrian expression is "mit Schlag" meaning "with whipped cream.") Frozen whipped topping is another item not available in Austria. We use a dry product, add milk, and beat to a thick, fluffy consistency.

Glazed Apple-Orange Bars

1 cup light brown sugar, packed
6 Tablespoons margarine
1/2 cup applesauce
1 teaspoon shredded orange peel
1 egg
1 teaspoon vanilla
1 1/4 cups flour
1 teaspoon baking powder
1/2 teaspoon salt
1/4 teaspoon baking soda
1/2 cup chopped walnuts
Orange Glaze (recipe below)

In a medium saucepan combine sugar and margarine; over low heat, stir until melted. Remove from heat. Blend in applesauce, orange peel, egg, and vanilla. In a separate bowl, combine the flour, baking powder, salt, and baking soda; gradually add to applesauce mixture. Add nuts and mix well. Spread in a greased 15x10x1 pan. Bake at 350º F for about 15 to 20 minutes or until it tests done (a wooden pick inserted in center comes out clean). Cool slightly. Drizzle with Glaze. Cool completely before cutting into bars or squares. Makes 24 bars (2 1/2 x 2 1/2 inches square).

Orange Glaze

1 1/2 cups sifted powdered sugar
1/2 teaspoon vanilla
2 to 2 1/2 Tablespoons
    orange juice

Combine all ingredients in a small bowl. Drizzle over warm bars.

Cook's Note: Especially moist and flavorful. Keeps well, too—if you can hide them from your family!

Jam Bars

1 1/2 cups flour
1 teaspoon baking powder
1 cup light brown sugar, packed
1/4 teaspoon salt
1 1/2 cups oatmeal
3/4 cup margarine, cut in 1/2
    inch pieces
1 1/2 cups jam (strawberry,
    raspberry, blackberry or apricot)

Mix together flour, baking powder, brown sugar, salt, and oatmeal. Using a pastry blender, or your nice clean fingers, cut in the margarine until mixture is crumbly.

Lightly spray a 9x13x2 pan with non-stick vegetable spray. Press 2/3 of mixture into pan. Spread jam gently over the top. Sprinkle with the reserved 1/3 of crumb mixture. Bake at 350º F for about 30 minutes. Cut into squares while still slightly warm, loosening around the edges of the pan also. Makes 18 to 24 bars.

Cook's Note: To make the jam easier to spread, place in a small microwave-safe bowl and heat for 10 to 15 seconds to soften. It goes on much more smoothly.

Jean Shannon's Crunch Bars (No Bake)

1/2 cup sugar
1 cup light corn syrup (or honey)
1 cup crunchy peanut butter
7 cups Rice Krispies cereal
1/2 cup semi-sweet chocolate
    chips

In a small saucepan combine sugar and corn syrup (or honey). Cook over medium heat until mixture comes to a full boil. Remove from heat; stir in peanut butter until it is melted.

Measure Rice Krispies into a large bowl. Pour syrup mixture slowly over cereal, mixing with a fork as you pour. Add chocolate chips; continue to stir until all is well blended and chips begin to melt.

Press mixture into a buttered 9x13x2 pan. Cool slightly and cut into squares. (Don't let it cool completely or it will be hard to cut.) Makes 30 squares.

Cook's Note: These easy NO BAKE treats are so good it is hard to stop after just one. Jean Shannon and her husband Bob are former Haus Edelweiss staff members. Since corn syrup is a product we cannot find in Austrian grocery stores, honey is used at the Haus. And when the stores stopped stocking Rice Krispies, we found that Special K makes a very acceptable substitute. (Creative cooks can ALWAYS find a way!)

Lemon Bars

2 cups flour
1/2 cup sifted powdered sugar
1 cup butter or margarine,
*   softened*
4 eggs
5 Tablespoons lemon juice
2 cups sugar
1/4 cup flour
1/2 teaspoon baking powder

In a small mixing bowl combine the flour, powdered sugar, and butter (or margarine). Make a crust by patting mixture into a 9x13x2 pan, flattening well to distribute evenly. Bake at 350º F for 25 minutes. Remove from oven.

While crust bakes, prepare lemon mixture. Using the same bowl, beat together the eggs, lemon juice, and sugar. Combine flour and baking powder; stir into liquids. Pour over hot crust. Bake at 350º F for 20 minutes. Cool before cutting. Dust lightly with sifted powdered sugar. Makes 24 bars (2 1/2 x 2 1/2 inches square).

Cook's Note: At the Haus we cut these into 15 larger pieces and serve on small individual plates for dinner dessert. (Line the plate with a small lace-paper doily for a festive presentation.)

Peanut Butter Bars

1/2 cup sugar
1/2 cup light brown sugar,
    packed
1/2 cup margarine, softened
1/3 cup creamy peanut butter
1 egg
1 teaspoon vanilla
1 cup flour
1/2 teaspoon baking soda
1/4 teaspoon salt
1 cup oatmeal
1 cup chocolate chips
Frosting (recipe below)

Cream thoroughly the sugar, brown sugar, margarine, and peanut butter; beat in the egg and vanilla. In a separate bowl, stir together the flour, baking soda, and salt; blend into creamed mixture. Add oatmeal, mixing well. Spread in a greased 9x13x2 pan. Sprinkle chocolate chips over the top. Bake at 350° F for 15 to 20 minutes. Spread with Frosting while still hot. Cool before cutting bars to desired size. Makes 24 bars (2 1/2 x 2 1/2 inches square).

Frosting

1 cup sifted powdered sugar
1 teaspoon margarine, softened
1/4 cup creamy peanut butter
3 Tablespoons milk
1 teaspoon vanilla

Mix together thoroughly to spreading consistency. Spread on hot bars.

Cook's Note: The combination of peanut butter and chocolate is a flavor hard to beat. Added to the Haus Edelweiss recipe file by former cook Lois Powney.

Zucchini Raisin Bars

*1 1/4 cups light brown sugar,
    packed*
1/2 cup margarine, softened
2 eggs
1 1/2 cups shredded zucchini
1 1/2 cups flour
1 teaspoon baking soda
1/2 teaspoon salt
1 teaspoon cinnamon
1 cup oatmeal
3/4 cup chopped walnuts
1 cup golden raisins

Cream together the brown sugar and margarine; add eggs and zucchini, beating well. In a separate bowl combine the flour, baking soda, salt, and cinnamon.

Remove 2 Tablespoons of dry ingredients; place in a small bowl and add nuts and raisins. Stir to coat. (This will keep the nuts from falling to the bottom of the batter.) Set aside.

Stir the remaining dry ingredients into the creamed mixture. Add oatmeal, nuts, and raisins with the mixture used to coat them. Blend well. Spread in a greased 15x10x1 pan. Bake at 350º F for about 20 minutes or until it tests done (a wooden pick inserted in center comes out clean). Cool.

Dust with sifted powdered sugar or drizzle with a simple glaze. For Glaze: blend 1 1/2 cups sifted powdered sugar with 2 to 3 Tablespoons milk to make a pourable mixture. Let glaze set before cutting into bars of desired size. Makes 24 bars (2 1/2 x 2 1/2 inches square).

Cook's Note: This recipe is the result of an over-abundance of zucchini in my garden several years ago. (Zucchini can be the cause of real desperation for gardeners searching for ways to make use of the Lord's bountiful provision!) Of several experiments, this was my family's favorite and it is now popular at Haus Edelweiss.

Deep Dish Brownies

3/4 cup margarine, melted
1 1/2 cups sugar
1 1/2 teaspoons vanilla
3 eggs
3/4 cup flour
1/2 cup cocoa
1/2 teaspoon baking powder
1/2 teaspoon salt

In a medium-sized bowl, beat together the melted margarine, sugar, and vanilla. Add eggs and beat well. In a separate bowl, stir together the flour, cocoa, baking powder, and salt. Gradually stir into the other ingredients, blending well.

Spread in a greased 8x8x2 inch baking pan. Bake at 350° F for 30 to 35 minutes, or until a wooden pick inserted in the middle comes out clean and brownies begin to pull away from the sides of the pan. Cool completely before cutting into squares. Makes 16 squares (2x2 inches each).

Cook's Note: Thick, fudgey, and WONDERFUL! A gem from a cookbook prepared by Owen County, Indiana Homemakers' Clubs.

Easy Brownies

1 cup margarine, melted
1 1/2 cups sugar
4 eggs
2 teaspoons vanilla
1 cup flour
6 Tablespoons cocoa
1/2 teaspoon salt

Beat together the margarine, sugar, eggs, and vanilla until well combined. In a separate bowl, stir together flour, cocoa, and salt. Add to creamed mixture and blend thoroughly. Pour into a greased 9x13x2 pan. Bake at 350º F for 20 to 25 minutes or until it tests done (a wooden pick inserted in center comes out clean). Do not over bake or product will be dry. Cool; cut into squares. Makes 18 to 24 brownies. If you like, dust with a bit of sifted powdered sugar before cutting.

Quick Chocolate No-Bakes

2 cups sugar
3 Tablespoons cocoa
1/2 cup milk
1/2 cup margarine
1/2 cup peanut butter
1 teaspoon vanilla
3 cups oatmeal

In a medium saucepan combine sugar, cocoa, milk, and margarine. Bring to a boil over medium heat; boil 1 minute. Remove from heat. Stir in peanut butter and vanilla. When peanut butter is melted, stir in oatmeal. Mix well. Line baking sheets with waxed paper or foil. Drop mixture by rounded teaspoonfuls. Cool completely. (While mixture is still hot cookies will tend to spread a bit. Push the edges back into shape with a spoon.) Makes about 4 dozen.

Cook's Note: Tony Twist, TCM's President, remembers his mom making these treats often when he was growing up.

Holiday Cookies

Learning about and experiencing the traditions of countries different from our own is part of the delight of living overseas. A holiday tradition in Austria is to give a gift to the people with whom one does business during the year—vendors, service people, bank, bakery, and other professional contacts. At Haus Edelweiss those gifts are products of the kitchen. Over the years, various cooks have elected to prepare bar cookies, candies, or sweet breads to give. More recently, trays of festive Christmas cookies have been given. Large round plastic trays which resemble cut glass are lined with lace paper doilies and about three dozen cookies are arranged in an attractive display. Once filled, the trays are covered with clear plastic wrap and tied with red ribbon. A gift card showing the Haus logo and bearing a Christmas greeting (hand written in German) is attached.

Twenty-five or more of these trays are prepared each year and delivered personally by members of the staff in early December, near December 6th when Austrians celebrate Saint Nicholas Day.

For two weeks in mid-November the Haus Edelweiss kitchen becomes a veritable cookie factory. Cookies for these gift trays are a selected group of varieties not made for regular meals or snacks. Usually six kinds are chosen with careful thought given to variety in shape, texture, flavor, and color. Recipes for six of those most often used are included in this section (Almond Crescents, Candy Cane Cookies, Cinnamon Stars, Honey Macaroonies, Mexican Wedding Cakes, Thumbprint Cookies). Sugar cookies cut into trees and bells are a frequent choice, also. Working on one variety at a time, cookies are baked, cooled on racks, then carefully packed into large airtight containers and stored in a freezer until time to assemble the trays.

Last year (1998) Jo and Marti turned out more than 1400 Christmas cookies— 118 dozen. Staff members, as always, were willing "taste testers," ensuring high quality control standards.

Almond Crescents

1/3 cup sugar
1 cup butter (or 1/2 cup butter and 1/2 cup margarine), softened
2/3 cup ground blanched almonds
1 2/3 cups flour
1/4 teaspoon salt
1 cup sifted powdered sugar
1 teaspoon cinnamon

Cream together the sugar, butter, and ground almonds. Stir together the flour and salt; gradually add to creamed mixture, blending well. CHILL DOUGH at least 1 hour. Meanwhile, stir together the powdered sugar and cinnamon in a shallow dish; set aside.

On a very lightly floured surface, roll small pieces of dough into pencil-sized strips with your hands. Cut into 2 1/2 inch lengths. Form into crescents on ungreased (or parchment paper-lined) baking sheets, spacing 1 1/2 to 2 inches apart. Bake at 325° F for about 12 to 14 minutes, until set but not brown. Remove to racks. While still slightly warm, carefully dip each cookie in the powdered sugar/cinnamon mixture. Cool on racks. Store air-tight. Makes 5 to 6 dozen.

Cook's Note: A traditional addition to the Christmas cookie tray.

Candy Cane Cookies

1 cup sifted powdered sugar
1 cup butter or margarine,
*   softened*
1 egg
1 1/2 teaspoons almond
*   flavoring*
1 teaspoon vanilla
2 1/2 cups flour
1/2 teaspoon salt
1/2 teaspoon red food coloring
1/3 cup finely crushed
*   peppermint sticks*
1/3 cup sugar

Cream together the powdered sugar and butter. Add egg, almond flavoring, and vanilla; blend well. Stir together flour and salt; gradually add to creamed mixture until well blended. Divide dough in half. To one half of the dough add the red food coloring, mixing until no trace of the lighter color remains. In a shallow dish combine crushed peppermint sticks and sugar; set aside.

On a lightly floured surface roll a scant teaspoonful of each color dough into a pencil-sized strip 4 inches long. Press strips lightly together and twist like a rope. Place on an ungreased (or parchment paper-lined) baking sheet. Curve the top down to form a hook. Continue, placing cookies about 2 inches apart.

Bake at 375° F for 6 to 7 minutes or until very lightly brown. Quickly remove to racks and while STILL HOT sprinkle with the peppermint mixture. (Set racks over waxed paper to catch the excess topping; it can be re-used.) Cool on racks. Take care! These are very fragile. Store airtight. Makes 4 dozen.

Cook's Note: A real touch of Christmas on your holiday cookie trays.

My first Christmas in Austria I was amazed to find that candy canes are not on the market. None! Not even peppermint sticks. This land of marvelous candy and no candy canes. (So guess what else I brought from the States?)

Cinnamon Stars

1 cup light brown sugar, packed
1/2 cup margarine, softened
1 egg
1 Tablespoon milk
1/4 cup finely chopped walnuts
2 cups flour
1/2 teaspoon cinnamon
1/8 teaspoon nutmeg
1/8 teaspoon cloves
pinch of salt (1/16 teaspoon)

Cream together the brown sugar and margarine; add eggs and milk, blending well. Stir in the nuts. Combine flour, cinnamon, nutmeg, cloves, and salt. Gradually add flour mixture to creamed mixture mixing thoroughly. CHILL DOUGH several hours or overnight.

Break off 1/4 of dough. (Return the rest to the refrigerator to stay firm.) Roll out on a lightly floured surface to 1/8 to 1/4 inch thickness. Cut with a star-shaped cookie cutter, dipped in flour from time to time for easy release. Repeat with remaining dough; scraps of dough can be re-rolled and cut. Place cookies 2 inches apart on lightly greased (or parchment paper-lined) baking sheets. Bake at 350° F for about 10 to 12 minutes or until pale brown. (The thicker the cookie, the longer the baking time required.) Cool on racks. Store airtight. Makes 5 dozen 3-inch cookies.

Cook's Note: These crisp, lightly spiced cookies are just right with a cup of hot tea. They keep well and can also be frozen.

Honey Macaroonies

1 1/2 cups oatmeal
1/2 cup flaked coconut
1/2 cup chopped walnuts
1/2 cup flour
3/4 cup light brown sugar,
    packed
1/2 cup butter or margarine
2 Tablespoons honey
18 red (or green) candied
    cherries, halved

Combine oatmeal, coconut, walnuts, and flour in a bowl. In a small heavy saucepan combine brown sugar, butter, and honey; bring to boiling. Pour syrup over dry ingredients and blend well. For each cookie, press 1 level Tablespoon of mixture into greased miniature muffin tins (1 1/2 to 1 3/4 inch size). Top each with a cherry half. Bake at 350° F for 15 to 18 minutes or until well browned. Cool in pans 10 minutes. Use the tip of a table knife to ease cookies from pans. Cool completely on racks. Store airtight. Makes about 3 dozen.

*Cook's Note: This recipe appeared years ago in **Better Homes and Gardens** magazine. The cookies are chewy and delicious, as well as a bit unusual. That prompted me to enter a plateful in the Indiana State Fair. The result was a blue ribbon.*

Mexican Wedding Cakes

1/2 cup sifted powdered sugar
1 cup butter, softened (no substitutes)
2 cups flour
1 Tablespoon vanilla (yes, Tablespoon)
1 cup finely chopped pecans
extra powdered sugar for rolling

Cream well the powdered sugar and softened butter. Mix in the flour gradually. Add vanilla and pecans; blend thoroughly.

Pinch off small pieces, not over 1 inch in diameter, and shape into balls. Place 1 inch apart on ungreased (or parchment paper-lined) baking sheets. Bake at 275° F for about 25 to 30 minutes (check after 20 minutes as ovens vary). Bake only until very light brown on the BOTTOM. Remove to racks. While still warm, gently shake a few at a time in a small bag of sifted powdered sugar. Finish cooling on racks. When completely cool, coat again with powdered sugar. Store airtight. Makes 4 dozen.

Cook's Note: This is my son Hank's longtime favorite Christmas cookie and a two-time Blue Ribbon winner at the Indiana State Fair. The cookies freeze very well.

Thumbprint Cookies

3/4 cup light brown sugar, packed
3/4 cup butter, softened
3/4 cup margarine
3 eggs, separated
1 1/2 teaspoons vanilla
3 cups flour
1/4 teaspoon salt
1 1/2 cups finely chopped walnuts
For centers, strawberry, cherry or raspberry jam (about 1 cup) or halved red candied cherries (about 45 whole)

Thoroughly cream brown sugar, butter, and margarine. Beat in egg YOLKS and vanilla. Stir together flour and salt; gradually add to creamed mixture, blending well.

In a small bowl, beat egg whites slightly. Shape cookie dough into SMALL (3/4 inch) balls; dip in egg white and roll in chopped nuts. Place 1 inch apart on ungreased (or parchment paper-lined) baking sheets. Before putting in the oven, make an indentation in the center of each cookie, almost to the bottom, using your thumb or finger. Bake at 375° F for 10 to 12 minutes until set and light brown. Cool on racks.

If the hollow has filled in during baking, gently press it again while cookies are still warm. In each cavity place a very small amount (1/2 teaspoon or less) of jam. Or use half of a candied cherry. Allow jam to dry a bit before storing. Store airtight with waxed paper between layers. Makes about 7 to 7 1/2 dozen.

Cook's Note: Delicious flavor, crunchy texture. A fine addition to any cookie plate or Christmas gift tray.

"You have made us feel paradise here, not only because of [the] excellent time of learning and vacation, but for the opportunity to see JESUS. We have seen Jesus in your lives, in your love, in your attitude and serving. We will never forget this orchard called Haus Edelweiss where Jesus is the vine and you are the fruitful branches. God bless you all."

Your Estonian brothers and sisters

Desserts

Onward Christian Soldiers

Service in the army of the King is a lifetime commitment. Enlistment is voluntary, made with the full knowledge that there is no program for automatic advancement through the ranks. There will be no cost-of-living raise, no longevity bonus, no cushy retirement plan at the end of twenty years. This is a "forever" deal. But FOREVER, eternity with Jesus, is the pension plan that awaits the servants of the King. The Medal of Honor each of us longs for is His "Well done, good and faithful servant."

Soldiers of this mighty band who come to Haus Edelweiss for training serve with a dedication and commitment that is humbling to behold. From throughout Central and Eastern Europe they come, men and women of all ages, traveling from as far north as Estonia, located on the Baltic sea just across the bay from Finland; from as far south as Macedonia and Bulgaria, nestled against the northern border of Greece; from as far east as the Ural Mountains in Russia. Often long and difficult, their journeys can take two-and-a-half to three days and require as many as five border crossings.

Eager and hungry to soak up more knowledge and increase their understanding of gospel truths, their appetites are insatiable. They long for MORE so that when they return to the front lines they will have much to share with their brothers and sisters in Christ. Voluminous notes are taken during the lectures each day. Upon returning home, some labor to organize and type the notes then travel from church to church in their area, teaching and sharing these precious insights into God's Word which reveal His plan for our lives.

The students who come to Haus Edelweiss are already in ministry, preaching, shepherding, and struggling to maintain their families. Economic conditions in most countries in Central and Eastern Europe are fragile; in some areas they are grim. Without the assistance of TCM through scholarships, this training—so urgently needed, so greatly desired—would be unattainable for them. Their expressions of gratitude toward the individuals and churches whose generosity makes it all possible are touching.

The instruction, study, and guidance offered during Leadership Training Conferences at Haus Edelweiss encourage and strengthen these church leaders, providing them with the training tools needed to help them grow in their service as missionaries, evangelists, counselors, shepherds, youth ministers, and church planters.

Apple Crunch

5 1/2 to 6 cups peeled,
*   sliced apples*
1/4 cup sugar
1/2 teaspoon cinnamon
1 cup flour
1 cup light brown sugar, packed
1/2 cup margarine, cut into
*   1/2-inch pieces*

Spread apples in a buttered 7x11 or 9-inch square baking dish. Combine sugar and cinnamon; sprinkle over apples. Combine flour and brown sugar; cut in butter with a pastry blender (or use your nice clean fingers) until mixture is crumbly. Sprinkle evenly over apples. Bake at 325º F for 50 to 60 minutes, until topping is golden brown. Serve warm or at room temperature. Serves 6.

Cook's Note: Wonderful with a scoop of vanilla ice cream.

Peach Crisp

2 cans (28 ounces each) peach
*   slices, drained*
2 Tablespoons sugar
1/2 teaspoon cinnamon
2 cups oatmeal
1 cup light brown sugar, packed
1/2 cup flour
2/3 cup margarine, melted

Spread drained peaches in a greased 9x13x2 baking pan. Combine sugar and cinnamon; sprinkle over peaches. Thoroughly mix oatmeal, brown sugar, and flour in a bowl. Stir in melted margarine to coat well. Scatter this crumbly mixture over peaches. Bake at 375º F for about 30 minutes, until topping is golden brown. Serve warm or at room temperature. Serves 12 to 15.

Cook's Note: Of course the perfect accompaniment is a scoop of vanilla ice cream.

Jo's Apple Crisp

*5 1/2 to 6 cups peeled and
    sliced apples*
1 cup flour
*3/4 to 1 cup sugar (depending
    on tartness of the apples)*
3/4 teaspoon salt
1 teaspoon baking powder
1 egg
1/3 cup vegetable oil
*1/2 teaspoon cinnamon
    (approximate)*

Place apple slices in a greased 7x11 baking dish. In a bowl combine the flour, sugar, salt, and baking powder. Make a well in the center; break the egg into the mixture. Blend with a fork until moistened and crumbly. (Use your nice clean hands to finish mixing if needed.)

Sprinkle topping evenly over the apples; drizzle oil over all. Sprinkle heavily with cinnamon. Bake at 350° F for about 45 minutes, until apples are tender and topping is crunchy. Serve warm. Enjoy! Serves 6.

Cook's Note: I picked this recipe from a rack in the grocery store in 1945. The recipe is supposed to serve 6, but the first time I served it for dinner, one serving was not enough. Before the evening was over my husband and I had emptied the pan! This is nearly as good as Apple Pie—and a lot quicker to prepare. A scoop of ice cream or a little "pour" cream makes a just-right finishing touch.

Fruit Cocktail "Cake"

2 cups sugar
2 teaspoons baking soda
2 cups flour
1/2 teaspoon salt
1/2 teaspoon allspice
1 teaspoon cinnamon
2 eggs, beaten
2 cups fruit cocktail, drained
  (reserve juice)
1/2 cup juice from fruit cocktail
1 teaspoon vanilla
3/4 cup shortening, softened
1 cup chopped nuts (optional)

Combine all ingredients except nuts in a large mixing bowl, beating well to combine thoroughly. Stir in nuts if used. Spread in a greased 9x13x2 pan. Bake at 350º F for about 35 minutes or until a rich brown color and product tests done (a wooden pick inserted in center comes out clean). Cool in pan. Serve with a generous dollop of whipped topping. Serves 12 to 15.

Cook's Note: Always served "mit Schlag" (with whipped cream).

Easy Chocolate Pudding Cake

1 box chocolate or chocolate
fudge cake mix, prepared
according to package
directions
1/2 cup chopped nuts (optional)
1/4 cup cocoa
1 cup sugar
2 1/4 cups hot water
1 teaspoon vanilla

Stir the nuts into the prepared cake batter. Pour batter into a greased 9x13x2 pan. Combine the cocoa and sugar; sprinkle evenly over the top of batter. Add vanilla to hot water; carefully pour over the batter. DO NOT STIR. Bake at 350º F for 35 to 40 minutes. Let stand 10 minutes. Best if served slightly warm. Serves 12 to 15.

Cook's Note: Serve plain or with a scoop of vanilla ice cream. Every gift deserves to be acknowledged, so this thank you is for Elaine Schultz for sharing this family favorite.

Applesauce Cake

1 1/3 cups sugar

1/2 cup + 1 Tablespoon
    margarine, softened

2 eggs

1 cup unsweetened applesauce

1 3/4 cups flour

1/2 teaspoon baking powder

1/2 teaspoon baking soda

1/4 teaspoon salt

1 teaspoon cinnamon

1/2 teaspoon cloves

1/2 cup chopped walnuts

In a large mixing bowl, thoroughly cream the sugar and margarine; add eggs and beat well. In a separate bowl, combine flour, baking powder, baking soda, salt, cinnamon, and cloves. On low speed or by hand, alternate adding the dry ingredients and applesauce to the creamed mixture, beginning and ending with dry ingredients. Stir in nuts. (Do not over mix.)

Turn into a greased and floured 7x11 pan (or a 9-inch square pan). Bake at 350º F for 45 to 55 minutes, until it tests done (a wooden pick inserted in center comes out clean, and cake begins to pull away from the sides of the pan). When cool, dust slightly with sifted powdered sugar. Makes 8 servings.

Cook's Note: To keep nuts from falling to the bottom of the cake while baking, remove 1 Tablespoon of the flour mixture and stir into the chopped nuts before adding the nuts to the batter. Make this ahead if you can. The flavor improves and the cake is more moist on the second day.

Chocolate Tweed Layer Cake

1/2 cup butter, softened
1 cup sugar, divided
1 teaspoon vanilla
2 cups sifted cake flour
3 teaspoons baking powder
dash of salt
1 cup milk
3 squares (1-ounce each)
    unsweetened chocolate,
    grated (large)
3 egg whites
Golden Butter Cream Frosting
    (recipe follows)
Chocolate Shadow
    (recipe follows)

In a large mixing bowl, cream together thoroughly the butter and 1/2 cup sugar. Beat in vanilla. Sift together flour, baking powder, and salt. Add to creamed mixture alternately with milk, beginning and ending with dry ingredients. Beat well after each addition. Stir chocolate into batter. In a separate bowl, beat egg whites until foamy; add remaining sugar, 1 Tablespoon at a time, and beat until whites form soft peaks. Gently fold whites into batter.

Grease 2 (9 inch) or 3 (8 inch) round cake pans and line the bottoms with waxed paper. Turn batter into pans, and bake at 350° F for 20 to 25 minutes, until cake begins to pull away from the sides of the pans and browns slightly (a wooden pick inserted in the center should come out clean). Do not over bake or cake will be dry. Cool in pans 5 minutes before turning out on wire racks to cool completely (remove waxed paper). Make Golden Butter Cream Frosting and spread between layers and on top and sides of cake. Partially freeze or refrigerate cake until completely cold before drizzling on Chocolate Shadow. Refrigerate leftovers (if any!).

Cake and frosting recipe reprinted with permission from **Women's Day** *Magazine.*

Golden Butter Cream Frosting

3/4 cup butter, softened
3 egg yolks
2 1/4 cups powdered sugar

Beat together butter and egg yolks. Gradually add sugar, beating until smooth.

Chocolate Shadow

1/2 cup (or a little less)
  semi-sweet chocolate chips
3 to 4 Tablespoons warm water

Melt chocolate in a double boiler or over low heat. Add warm water to make thin enough to pour. Drizzle across top and down sides of chilled cake.

Cook's Note: Slightly softening the chocolate in a microwave will make grating it easier. Avoid handling the grated chocolate so the shreds don't break up too much. If the chocolate is too fine, the cake will not have the desired tweedy appearance, texture, or taste. This cake can also be made in a 9x13x2 pan.

Sometimes the dishes we prepare, particularly those we reserve for special occasions, have a story to tell. Chocolate Tweed Cake is one of those. It is staff member Tracy Bergin's story:

"My Mom clipped this recipe from a 1967 Woman's Day magazine, and it has become a family tradition. I always requested it for my birthday, and when Lewis and I decided to get married I knew it had to be the wedding cake as well. Now I enjoy making it on my birthday to share with my colleagues at Haus Edelweiss, though many of the ingredients (unsweetened baking chocolate and cake flour for example) are not available here and must be brought from the States."

When Tracy's April birthday occurs during a conference, she recruits husband Lewis to help with grating the chocolate and she prepares enough 9x13 cakes to serve this luscious treat for dinner dessert.

Chocolate Chocolate Chip Cake

1 box chocolate fudge cake mix
1 package (3 ounce) chocolate
  fudge instant pudding mix
1 cup sour cream
1/2 cup vegetable oil
2/3 cup water
4 eggs
1/2 cup semi-sweet chocolate
  chips

Combine all ingredients except chocolate chips in large mixing bowl. Beat at medium speed 4 minutes, scraping sides of the bowl often. Batter will be very thick. Fold in chocolate chips.

Turn into a greased and floured 12-cup bundt pan. Bake at 350º for about 55 minutes, until a wooden pick inserted between the rim of a pan and the tube comes out clean. Cool in pan 10 minutes before turning out on rack to cool. When cool, lightly sift a little powdered sugar over the top if desired. Serves 14 to 16.

Cook's Note: For Commencement Sunday, graduates are encouraged to invite their families for the morning worship service and graduation ceremony, as well as the dinner which follows. In April 1998 the IBS (TCM's Institute for Biblical Studies based at Haus Edelweiss) graduated 16 students (6 from Romania, 6 from Hungary, 2 from Poland, and 2 from Estonia). At dinner, we served 93 people. The dessert was Chocolate Chocolate Chip Cake, baked in 9x13x2 pans and frosted with Chocolate Butter Cream Frosting. Though there were 8 cakes (a total of 120 pieces) not a crumb was left. Thanks for this crowd-pleaser goes to Carolyn Gindling, part of my extended family who loves chocolate as much as I do.

Chocolate Zucchini Cake

1 1/2 cups sugar
1/2 cup margarine, softened
1/2 cup vegetable oil
2 eggs, slightly beaten
1/2 cup buttermilk
1 teaspoon vanilla
2 1/2 cups flour
1/4 cup cocoa
1 teaspoon baking soda
1/2 teaspoon baking powder
1/2 teaspoon salt
1/2 teaspoon cinnamon
1/4 teaspoon cloves
2 cups shredded zucchini
1/2 cup chocolate chips
1/2 cup chopped nuts (optional)

Cream together the sugar, margarine, and oil. Add eggs, buttermilk, and vanilla, beating well. In another bowl, combine flour, cocoa, baking soda, baking powder, salt, cinnamon, and cloves. Gradually stir into creamed mixture. Add zucchini and blend thoroughly. Spread in a greased 9x13x2 pan. Sprinkle with chocolate chips and nuts. Bake at 350° for 35 to 40 minutes or until a wooden pick inserted in center comes out clean, and cake begins to pull away from the sides of the pan. Serves 12 to 15.

Cook's Note: This may also be baked in a bundt pan. It doesn't really need a frosting. From another cook seeking ways to use surplus zucchini from the garden (in **Bountiful Harvest Cookbook**_)._

Reprinted with permission from **Bountiful Harvest**, _Reiman Publishing_

Coronation Cake

1 1/2 cups sugar
1 cup butter
2 eggs
1 teaspoon vanilla
1 bottle (2 ounces) red food
    coloring
2 1/2 cups cake flour
1 teaspoon salt
1 teaspoon baking soda
2 Tablespoons cocoa
1 cup buttermilk
1 Tablespoon vinegar

In a large mixing bowl, thoroughly cream the sugar and butter until light and fluffy. Add eggs, vanilla, and red food coloring; beat to blend completely. Stir together the cake flour, salt, baking soda, and cocoa. Set aside. Stir vinegar into buttermilk. Add dry ingredients to the creamed mixture alternately with the buttermilk, beginning and ending with dry ingredients. (About 1/4 of flour at each addition and about 1/3 of buttermilk works well.) Blend well. Pour into a greased and floured 9x13x2 pan. Bake at 350° F for about 35 minutes or until cake tests done when checked with a wooden pick and just begins to pull away from the sides of the pan. Cool completely on a rack before frosting.

Frost with a fluffy white frosting, such as Bakery Style "Whipped Cream" Frosting (recipe in this section). Makes 15 servings.

Cook's Note: This cake is a really lovely dark red color with a moist, flavorful texture. The rich red color of the cake contrasted with the white frosting made this an especially festive addition to the dessert menu the year our Jause (see International Foods section) occurred on Valentine's Day.

About Cakes

One of the few foods not always "made from scratch" at Haus Edelweiss is cake. With the exception of Applesauce Cake, Chocolate Zucchini Cake, and a few special-occasion cakes for which you will find recipes in this book, we rely on boxed cake mixes. When six or seven 9x13 cakes are needed per meal, time and labor are major considerations. Cake mixes are a real boon for the busy cook.

Since Austrians are not into "quickie" processed foods to the extent that most Americans are, you will not find US-style boxed cake mixes on the shelves in grocery stores here. Helpful and generous short-term workers (our wonderful STWs) pack the boxes into their suitcases and carry them over for us—no small thing considering that a minimum of six boxes of any one flavor is needed to prepare dessert for one dinner. Some of those suitcases get really heavy! Churches or individuals sometimes send one or more cases (of twelve boxes). What a help! We accept them with heartfelt gratitude and appreciation.

Create-A-Cake from a Mix

A bit bored with the standard cake mix choices in your pantry? Try one of these combinations for a little variety. Mix as directed on the box:

Maple-Nut Cake

1 box yellow cake mix
2 teaspoons maple flavoring
1/2 cup finely chopped pecans

Minty Chocolate Cake

1 box dark chocolate
*   fudge cake mix*
1/2 teaspoon peppermint flavor-

Applesauce Walnut Cake

1 box spice cake
1 cup finely chopped walnuts
Substitute 1 jar or can (15
*   ounces) applesauce for the water*

Bakery Style "Whipped Cream" Frosting

2 1/2 Tablespoons cornstarch
1 teaspoon sugar
1 1/2 cups milk
1 cup sugar
1/2 cup shortening
1/2 cup margarine
1 teaspoon vanilla (or almond)
    flavoring
dash of salt

In a small saucepan, combine the cornstarch, 1 teaspoon sugar, and milk. Cook and stir over medium heat until mixture boils and thickens. Transfer to a bowl, cover and refrigerate to CHILL THOROUGHLY.

In a small mixing bowl, beat the 1 cup sugar, shortening, and margarine until VERY light and fluffy—about 10 minutes. Add the vanilla, salt, and the cold cooked mixture. Continue beating well until mixed and very fluffy—about 3 to 5 minutes more. Frosts a 9x13 cake.

Cook's Note: Store frosted cake in a cool place until ready to serve. Refrigerate leftovers.

Coconut Pecan Frosting

2/3 cup sugar
2/3 cup evaporated milk
2 egg yolks
1/3 cup butter or margarine
1 1/3 cups (3 1/2-ounce can)
    flaked coconut
1 cup chopped pecans
1/2 teaspoon vanilla

In a medium saucepan combine the sugar, evaporated milk, egg yolks, and butter. Cook and stir over medium heat until mixture comes to a boil. Remove from heat. Stir in coconut, nuts, and vanilla. Stir well until thick. Frosts a 9x13 cake.

Cook's Note: The classic frosting for German Chocolate Cake, the favorite of Lennie Sutton, long-time Haus Edelweiss staff member.

Cream Cheese Frosting

2 packages (3 ounces each)
cream cheese at room
temperature
6 Tablespoons butter or
margarine, softened
3 cups sifted powdered sugar
1 teaspoon vanilla

Cream together the cream cheese and butter. Gradually mix in the powdered sugar. Add vanilla and blend well until smooth. Frosts a 9x13 cake.

Cook's Note: Need to frost more than one cake for a party? Here are the quantities needed to frost four 9x13x2 cakes, or three 10x15x1 cakes:

3 packages (8 ounces each) cream cheese
1 1/2 cups margarine, softened
3 pounds (about 13 1/2 cups) sifted pow-
dered sugar
1 Tablespoon vanilla

Prepare as directed above.

Chocolate Cream Cheese Frosting

Prepare as for Cream Cheese Frosting, substituting 1/4 cup cocoa (sifted if needed) for 1/4 cup of the powdered sugar.

Mock Whipped Cream Frosting

1 cup sugar
1/2 cup margarine, softened
1/2 cup shortening
1 egg yolk
1/2 cup cold milk
1 teaspoon vanilla (or almond)
    flavoring
dash of salt

Combine all ingredients in a small mixing bowl. Beat on high speed for 6 to 8 minutes, or until sugar is dissolved and mixture is the consistency of thick whipped cream. (Check for any graininess by putting a small amount on the tip of your tongue and tasting it. If some sugar is still undissolved, continue beating.) Spread on completely cooled cake. Generously frosts a 9x13 cake.

Cook's Note: Be sure to refrigerate frosted cake.

Vanilla Butter Cream Frosting

3 cups sifted powdered sugar
1/3 cup butter or margarine,
    softened
1 1/2 teaspoons vanilla flavoring
2 Tablespoons milk

In a small mixing bowl beat together the powdered sugar and butter to blend. Stir in vanilla and milk to a smooth spreading consistency. If necessary, add a little more milk, 1 teaspoon at a time, to reach desired consistency. Frosts a 9x13 cake.

Orange Butter Cream Frosting

3 cups sifted powdered sugar
1/3 cup butter or margarine,
softened
2 Tablespoons orange juice
2 teaspoons grated orange peel

In a small mixing bowl beat together the powdered sugar and butter to blend. Stir in orange juice and grated orange peel to a smooth spreading consistency. If necessary, add a little more juice, 1 teaspoon at a time, to reach desired consistency. Frosts a 9x13 cake.

Peanut Butter Cream Frosting

3 cups sifted powdered sugar
1/3 cup creamy peanut butter
1 1/2 teaspoons vanilla flavoring
1/4 to 1/3 cup milk

In a small mixing bowl beat together the powdered sugar and peanut butter to blend. Stir in vanilla and milk to a smooth spreading consistency. If necessary, add a little more milk, 1 teaspoon at a time, to reach desired consistency. Frosts a 9x13 cake.

Chocolate Butter Cream Frosting

3 3/4 cups sifted powdered sugar
1/4 cup + 1 Tablespoon cocoa
1/2 cup butter or margarine,
*   softened*
6 Tablespoons evaporated milk
1 Tablespoon vanilla

Sift the powdered sugar and cocoa together. Combine all ingredients in a small mixing bowl and beat until smooth and creamy. (If necessary, a small amount of evaporated milk may be added.) Frosts a 15x10 pan of brownies.

Cook's Note: If you are frosting a 9x13 cake, the extra frosting will keep in the refrigerator for up to 2 weeks (assuming, of course, that there are not some willing "tasters" at your Haus eager to help you out). For larger quantities, two times this recipe will frost three 9x13 cakes.

Dark Chocolate Sauce

1/2 cup cocoa
1 1/4 cups sugar
1/8 teaspoon salt
1 cup evaporated milk
1/4 cup margarine, cut in
    chunks
1 teaspoon vanilla

In a heavy-bottom saucepan, combine the cocoa, sugar, and salt. Blend in evaporated milk; add margarine. Cook over medium heat, stirring constantly, until mixture boils. Boil 2 minutes. Remove from heat; stir in vanilla. Stir sauce occasionally as it cools to incorporate the thickening layer on top. When completely cool, pour into a jar with a tight-fitting lid. Refrigerate. Keeps for a month or more. Makes about 2 1/4 cups.

Cook's Note: Ice cream with Chocolate Sauce is the traditional Sunday-supper dessert at Haus Edelweiss. The Austrians have developed ice cream making to a fine art and few people can pass up this favorite. The taste for ice cream knows no international boundaries.

"Dear friends!

*We fall in love with you from first sight. We are
so grateful to you that you invited us to this
Paradise on Earth. Your Haus Edelweiss is so
wonderful!"*

Group from Ukraine

*Cooking
for a
Crowd*

An Experience to Treasure

   The highlight of the academic year at Haus Edelweiss is Commencement. Usually the third or fourth Sunday in April, it is a very special and exciting time. Graduating Master of Arts and Certificate students, many accompanied by family members, arrive on Saturday. Dinnertime on Saturday evening is filled with the happy buzz of eager anticipation, much like a room of excited children on Christmas Eve.

   Friends of the graduates are welcome to join us on Sunday morning for worship service, and share in the joy as degrees are awarded and certificates presented. All who come are also invited to the dinner which follows. At that time, all three dining rooms are filled to capacity with 90 or more people, and additional tables are set up as needed in the adjacent lounge area.

   Although crowded and hectic, it is a time spilling over with laughter and warm fellowship. Conversation and general chatter flow across the tables with Czech, Hungarian, Russian, Romania, Polish, and Estonian layered over the English. A bountiful and festive dinner (savory pork roast, creamy potatoes, vegetable, and salad) disappears and is topped off by a luscious dessert.

   Finally, after the graduates have posed for their group photograph and dozens of cameras have recorded special "Kodak moments," the crowd begins to thin and guests pack up for the long journey home. Hugs and handshakes are shared, words of blessing given and received. The last of the travelers is waved down the driveway by a cluster of tired Americans. As we turn back to the Haus, we assure each other that this has (again) been an experience to treasure.

Easy Minestrone Soup

	50 SERVINGS	75 SERVINGS
ground beef	2 1/4 pounds	3 1/2 pounds
beef broth	12 cans (14 oz each)	18 cans (14 oz each)
canned tomatoes, cut up	3 cans (29 oz each)	5 cans (29 oz each)
instant beef bouillon	3 Tablespoons	4 1/2 Tablespoons
basil	1 Tablespoon	1 1/2 Tablespoons
oregano	1 Tablespoon	1 1/2 Tablespoons
garlic powder	3/4 teaspoon	1 1/4 teaspoons
frozen mixed vegetables	3 3/4 pounds	5 1/2 pounds
cooked, drained small white (navy) beans	12 cups	18 cups

In a large kettle, cook the meat until it loses all its pink color, breaking up clumps as it cooks. Add all the rest of the ingredients EXCEPT beans. Bring to a boil; reduce heat, cover and simmer 1 to 1 1/2 hours. Add the beans; heat thoroughly.

Cook's Note: Lots of vegetables and not a lot of broth. Add more broth if you like a less dense soup.

Peasant Bean Soup

	60 SERVINGS	90 SERVINGS
dry red kidney beans	3 1/4 pounds	5 1/4 pounds
dry pinto beans	3 1/4 pounds	5 1/4 pounds
dry small white (navy) beans	2 1/4 pounds	3 3/4 pounds
lentils	1 pound	1 1/2 pounds
carrots, sliced into rounds	9 large	13 to 14 large
onion, diced	2 1/2 cups	3 3/4 cups
celery, thinly sliced	3 cups	4 1/2 cups
canned tomatoes, cut up, with juice	12 cups	18 cups
garlic powder	3 teaspoons	4 teaspoons
pepper	1 1/2 teaspoons	2 1/4 teaspoons
cooked smoked ham, diced	3 pounds	4 1/2 pounds
salt to taste		

Rinse red, pinto, and white beans. Place in a large kettle and cover completely with cold water; soak overnight.

Drain beans; return to kettle and cover with fresh water. Bring to a boil; lower heat and simmer 1 to 1 1/2 hours. Add lentils, carrots, onion, and celery. Continue cooking over low heat until beans are tender, adding more water if necessary. Add tomatoes, seasonings (including salt to taste), and diced ham. Simmer another 30 minutes.

Bar-B-Q Hamburger on Buns

	50 SERVINGS	75 SERVINGS
ground beef	12 pounds	18 pounds
onion, chopped	4 1/2 cups	7 1/2 cups
salt	4 Tablespoons	6 Tablespoons
chili powder	6 Tablespoons	9 Tablespoons
pepper	2 Tablespoons	3 Tablespoons
dry mustard	3 teaspoons	4 1/2 teaspoons
catsup	2 cups	3 cups
water	8 cups	12 cups
vinegar	4 Tablespoons	6 Tablespoons
brown sugar, packed	6 Tablespoons	1/2 cup + 1 Tablespoon
quick-cooking oatmeal	2 cups	3 cups
hamburger buns, split	50	75

Brown ground beef and onion together in a large, heavy kettle, breaking up clumps of meat as it cooks. Stir in salt, chili powder, and pepper. Cook 5 minutes longer. Add dry mustard, catsup, water, vinegar, and brown sugar. Bring to a boil. Add oatmeal, mixing well. Reduce heat; simmer 45 to 60 minutes, stirring occasionally to prevent sticking. Serve on hamburger buns. Allow about 1/3 cup per serving.

Cook's Note: Great for a church supper, family reunion, or a late New Year's Eve party. Serve with pickles, a crisp veggie tray, Creamy Slaw, and potato chips.

Pizza Burgers

	50 SERVINGS	100 SERVINGS
ground beef, cooked and drained of fat	4 1/2 pounds	9 pounds
luncheon meat (any kind)	2 1/2 pounds	5 pounds
American cheese	1 1/2 pounds	3 pounds
salt	1 Tablespoon	2 Tablespoons
leaf sage	1 Tablespoon	2 Tablespoons
oregano	2 1/2 Tablespoons	5 Tablespoons
parsley flakes	1/4 cup	1/2 cup
pizza sauce, spaghetti sauce or tomato sauce	7 1/2 cups	14 to 15 cups (1 no. 10 can)
hamburger buns, split	50	100

While the ground beef cooks, grind together the luncheon meat and cheese. Combine cooked meat, ground luncheon meat and cheese, seasonings, and pizza sauce. Mix well. Use a #12 scoop (scant 1/3 cup) to place mixture on the bottom half of each bun. Top with other half. Arrange on baking sheets and cover lightly with foil. Bake at 400° to 425° F for about 12 minutes to heat through.

Calico Salad

	50 SERVINGS	*75 SERVINGS*
canned green beans, drained	*5 cans (29 oz each)*	*2 no. 10 cans (about 105 oz each)*
canned whole kernel corn, drained	*5 cans (29 oz each)*	*2 no. 10 cans (about 105 oz each)*
red kidney beans, rinsed and drained	*7 cans (29 oz each)*	*3 no. 10 cans (about 105 oz each)*
onion, diced fine	*5 Tablespoons*	*1/2 cup*
green pepper, chopped	*3 cups*	*5 cups*
sugar	*4 cups*	*6 cups*
oil	*2 cups*	*3 cups*
vinegar	*2 cups*	*3 cups*

Combine drained green beans, corn, and kidney beans in a large bowl. Add onion and chopped green pepper and combine. In a separate bowl, whisk together sugar, oil, and vinegar for dressing. Pour over vegetables; blend well. Place in a covered container and REFRIGERATE OVERNIGHT to marinate. Stir well before serving with a slotted spoon to drain excess marinade.

Cook's Note: Can be made ahead as it keeps well in the refrigerator for a week or more.

Green Pea and Cheese Salad

	50 SERVINGS	75 SERVINGS
vegetable oil	1 1/2 cups	2 1/4 cups
lemon juice	3/4 cup	1 1/8 cups
garlic powder	3/4 teaspoon	1 1/8 teaspoons
dill weed	1 Tablespoon	1 1/2 Tablespoons
thyme leaves, crushed	1 1/2 teaspoons	2 1/4 teaspoons
salt	1 1/2 Tablespoons	2 1/4 Tablespoons
pepper	3/4 teaspoon	1 1/8 teaspoons
frozen peas, thawed	7 1/2 pounds	11 pounds
celery, thinly sliced	3 cups	4 1/2 cups
onion, finely minced	2 cups	3 cups
American, Monterey Jack or Swiss cheese, cut in 1/2 inch cubes	12 cups	18 cups

Whisk together the oil, lemon juice, garlic powder, dill weed, thyme, salt, and pepper to make the dressing. Pour over the thawed peas in a large bowl; toss to coat well. Add celery, onion, and cheese cubes. Toss again to blend completely. REFRIGERATE 2 or more hours to blend flavors and chill well.

Homestead Salad

	50 SERVINGS	75 SERVINGS
frozen mixed vegetables	5 1/2 pounds	8 1/4 pounds
celery, diced (optional)	4 ribs	6 ribs
green pepper, diced	4 medium	6 medium
onion, finely diced	2 cups	3 cups
red kidney beans, rinsed and drained	4 cans (26-30 oz each)	6 cans (26-30 oz. each)
sugar	3 cups	4 1/2 cups
flour	3/4 cup	1 1/8 cups
dry mustard	4 teaspoons	6 tablespoons
cider vinegar	2 cups	3 cups

Cook frozen mixed vegetables in boiling salted water until tender-crisp; drain well. Combine with other vegetables in a large bowl. While vegetables are cooking, make dressing by combining sugar, flour, and dry mustard in a medium saucepan. Whisk in vinegar. Cook over medium heat, stirring constantly, until mixture boils and thickens. Lower heat; cook 1 or 2 minutes longer. Pour hot mixture over vegetables.

Put mixture into covered container; REFRIGERATE OVERNIGHT to marinate. Stir well before serving.

Cook's Note: Keeps well in the refrigerator. Tangy taste with a nice crunch.

Rotini Vegetable Salad

	50 SERVINGS	75 SERVINGS
frozen cauliflower-broccoli mix, thawed	6 cups	9 cups
salt	to taste	to taste
medium carrots, sliced 1/4 inch thick	5 to 6	8 to 9
small (4 to 6 inch) zucchini, sliced thin	5 to 6	8 to 9
small onions, sliced paper thin	5 (about 1 1/2 cups)	8 (about 2 1/4 cups)
frozen peas, thawed	1 1/2 cups	2 1/4 cups
canned mushroom slices, drained	3 cans (8 oz each)	5 cans (8 oz each)
Rotini (spiral macaroni), cooked, rinsed and drained	2 pounds (32 ozs)	3 pounds (54 ozs)

Dressing

	50 SERVINGS	75 SERVINGS
mayonnaise	1 1/2 cups	2 1/4 cups
Italian dressing	1 1/2 cups	2 1/4 cups
sour cream	1 1/2 cups	2 1/4 cups
Italian seasoning (herb mix)	1 1/2 teaspoons	2 1/4 teaspoons

Sprinkle the thawed cauliflower-broccoli lightly with salt. Parboil carrots: In a saucepan, place carrots and just enough water to cover; bring to a boil over high heat and cook just 1 MINUTE. Remove from heat; drain and rinse with cold water to stop cooking. Drain again.

In a large bowl toss together all the vegetables and the Rotini. Combine dressing ingredients, blending well. Pour dressing over vegetables and Rotini; toss to coat well. Taste for salt. Cover and CHILL 2 hours or longer before serving.

Sauerkraut Salad

	50 SERVINGS	75 SERVINGS
sauerkraut, rinsed and drained thoroughly	6 cans (26-30 oz each)	9 cans (26-30 oz each)
celery, chopped	6 cups	9 cups
onion, chopped	3 cups	4 1/2 cups
red or green pepper, chopped	4 1/2 cups	6 3/4 cups
sugar	6 cups	9 cups
oil	2 cups	3 cups
vinegar	2 cups	3 cups

Squeeze any remaining liquid from the sauerkraut. Combine with celery, onion, and green pepper. In a separate bowl, whisk together sugar, oil, and vinegar. Pour dressing over vegetables; mix well. Cover and refrigerate overnight or longer. Mix well before serving.

Cook's Note: The flavor improves with standing so try to make this tasty, crunchy salad two or three days in advance if possible.

Turkey Salad

	50 SERVINGS	75 SERVINGS
cooked, diced turkey breast	24 cups	36 cups
hard cooked eggs, diced	18	27
celery, diced	6 cups	9 cups
dill pickle, diced	3 cups	4 1/2 cups
crisp apple, peeled and diced fine or shredded	6 small	9 small
mayonnaise	6 cups	9 cups
onion, minced	1/4 cup	1/3 cup
lemon juice	2 Tablespoons	3 Tablespoons
salt (or to taste)	2 Tablespoons	3 Tablespoons
pepper	3/4 teaspoon	1 1/8 teaspoons

In a large bowl combine turkey, eggs, celery, dill pickle, and apples. Blend together the mayonnaise, onion, lemon juice, salt, and pepper. Pour over turkey mixture; blend thoroughly. Taste for salt. If needed, add a little more mayonnaise. CHILL several hours or overnight to blend flavors.

Meat Loaf

	50 SERVINGS	75 SERVINGS
eggs	14	24
milk	4 2/3 cups	6 2/3 cups
salt	2 Tablespoons + 1 teaspoon	3 Tablespoons + 1 teaspoon
pepper	1 3/4 teaspoons	2 1/2 teaspoons
onion powder	1 3/4 teaspoons	2 1/2 teaspoons
fine dry bread crumbs	4 2/3 cups	6 2/3 cups
hamburger	15 1/2 pounds	22 1/2 pounds

Beat eggs; add milk, salt, pepper, onion powder, and the dry bread crumbs. Stir to blend well; let stand about 5 minutes until liquid is absorbed. Add the hamburger and mix very thoroughly. (Unless you have a large-capacity, heavy-duty mixer, it is best to work with 1/2 or 1/3 of these quantities at a time. Divide the liquid/crumb mixture into 2 or 3 large bowls. Divide the hamburger in the same way and mix with your hands, taking care to mix thoroughly.)

Form into loaf shapes, patting and shaping firmly so it will hold its shape well. Place in shallow baking pans (about 2 inches deep to catch drippings). Tent foil loosely over the top of the pans. Bake at 350º F for about 1 3/4 hours. Remove foil during the last half hour. Let loaves stand in pans for 10 minutes to firm up before removing and slicing.

Yield	6 loaves	10 loaves

Baked Beef and Rigatoni

	50 SERVINGS	75 SERVINGS
lean ground beef	6 pounds	9 pounds
onion, chopped	3 cups	4 1/2 cups
green pepper, diced	2 cups	3 cups
canned Italian-style tomatoes, cut up	18 cups	27 cups
tomato sauce	6 cups	9 cups
tomato paste	4 1/2 cups	6 3/4 cups
water	4 1/2 cups	6 3/4 cups
canned sliced mushrooms, with juice	3 cans (8 oz each)	5 cans (8 oz each)
garlic powder	3/4 teaspoon	1 1/8 teaspoons
sugar	4 Tablespoons	6 Tablespoons
dried oregano	2 Tablespoons	3 Tablespoons
salt	3 Tablespoons	4 1/2 Tablespoons
pepper	1 1/2 teaspoons	2 1/4 teaspoons
parsley flakes	2 1/2 Tablespoons	3 3/4 Tablespoons
Rigatoni	2 1/4 pounds	3 1/3 pounds
eggs, slightly beaten	12	18
small curd cottage cheese	3 pounds	4 1/2 pounds
grated Parmesan cheese	3 cups	4 1/2 cups

Cook together the ground beef, onion, and green pepper, breaking up meat as it cooks, until meat is done and onion transparent. Add tomatoes, tomato sauce, tomato paste, water, mushrooms with juice, and all the seasonings. Bring to a boil. Lower heat and simmer 1 1/2 hours. Remove from heat.

Cook Rigatoni in boiling, salted water. Drain and KEEP HOT.

In a large bowl, mix together the beaten eggs, cottage cheese, and Parmesan cheese. Add the hot cooked Rigatoni and mix together thoroughly. Spoon mixture into greased baking pans. Top with tomato-meat sauce. Bake at 350° F for 45 to 60 minutes or until heated through. When using larger pans, increase baking time somewhat. If desired, sprinkle with some additional Parmesan cheese.

Pan sizes	6 pans (9x13x2) or 3 pans (12x18)	9 pans (9x13x2) or 4 pans (12x18)

Chicken Rice Casserole

	50 SERVINGS	75 SERVINGS
onion, finely diced	3 cups	4 1/2 cups
celery, finely diced	3 cups	4 1/2 cups
margarine	2 3/4 cups	4 cups
flour	2 2/3 cups	4 cups
chicken broth	9 1/2 cups	15 3/4 cups
milk	8 1/4 cups	12 cups
evaporated milk	7 1/2 cups	11 1/4 cups
salt	2 Tablespoons	3 Tablespoons
cooked, diced chicken breast	24 cups	36 cups
cooked rice	16 1/4 cups	24 cups
canned sliced mushrooms, drained and chopped	5 cans (8 oz each)	9 cans (8 oz each)
shredded cheese	2 pounds (7 1/2 cups)	3 pounds (11 1/2 cups)
rich cracker crumbs	5 1/4 cups	8 cups

In a large kettle, sauté onion and celery in margarine until transparent. Remove from heat; whisk in flour until smooth. Blend in chicken broth; return to heat and bring to a boil, stirring to prevent sticking. Add milk, evaporated milk, and salt. Cook, stirring constantly, until mixture comes to a boil. Lower heat and simmer one minute. Remove from heat and mix in chicken, rice, and mushrooms. Taste for salt.

Spoon mixture into greased baking pans. Sprinkle top with shredded cheese and then crumbs. Bake at 350° F until hot through and bubbly at edges (about 30 to 45 minutes). Topping should be lightly browned all over.

Pan sizes	6 pans (9x13x2) or 3 pans (12x18)	9 pans (9x13x2) or 4 pans (12x18)

Cook's Note: When baking multiple pans of food in one oven, a little longer cooking time may be required.

Tuna at its Best

	50 SERVINGS	75 SERVINGS
cream of mushroom soup,	9 cans	13 cans
undiluted milk	4 1/2 cups	6 1/2 cups
mayonnaise	4 1/2 cups	6 1/2 cups
onion powder	1 1/2 teaspoons	2 1/4 teaspoons
pepper	2 1/4 teaspoons	3 1/4 teaspoons
chunk tuna, drained and chopped	5 cans (13 oz each)	7 cans (13 oz each)
shredded Monterey Jack cheese	4 1/2 cups (18 oz)	6 1/2 cups (26 oz)
canned mushroom slices, drained and chopped	4 cans (8 oz each)	6 cans (8 oz each)
frozen peas, thawed	9 cups	13 cups
medium noodles, cooked and drained	3 1/3 pounds	4 3/4 pounds
crushed potato chips	6 3/4 cups	9 3/4 cups

Thoroughly combine mushroom soup, milk, mayonnaise, onion powder, and pepper in a large bowl. Blend in tuna, cheese, mushrooms, and peas. Add the cooked, drained noodles and combine thoroughly. Spread mixture into greased pans. Top with crushed potato chips. Bake at 350° F for 30 to 40 minutes or until mixture is hot all the way through.

Pan sizes	6 pans (9x13x2) or 3 pans (12x18)	9 pans (9x13x2) or 4 pans (12x18)

Cook's Note: Larger pans will require about 1 hour baking time. Check center to be certain it is hot through.

Turkey Tetrazini

	50 SERVINGS	75 SERVINGS
onion, finely diced	1 1/2 cups	2 1/4 cups
margarine	3/4 cup	1 1/4 cups
flour	2/3 cup	1 cup + 1 1/2 Tablespoons
salt to taste	about 3 teaspoons	about 5 teaspoons
pepper	3/4 teaspoon	1 1/4 teaspoons
parsley flakes	1 1/2 teaspoons	2 1/2 teaspoons
chicken or turkey broth	6 cups	10 cups
milk	3 cups	5 cups
evaporated milk	3 cups	5 cups
canned sliced mushrooms, drained	3 cans (8 oz each)	5 cans (8 oz each)
spaghetti, cooked and drained	2 2/3 pounds (40 oz)	4 1/3 pounds (70 oz)
cooked turkey breast, diced	15-18 cups	25-30 cups
shredded cheese (Monterey Jack or cheddar)	6 cups (1 1/2 pounds)	10 cups (2 1/2 pounds)

Sauté onion in margarine until transparent. Whisk in flour, salt, pepper, and parsley flakes, stirring until smooth. Remove from heat; add broth and blend well. Cook over medium heat, stirring frequently, until mixture almost boils. Add milk; bring almost to a boil again, then add evaporated milk. (Adding the liquids in smaller amounts this way works much better with larger quantities as the temperature of the cooked mixture is not reduced so sharply.) When sauce again returns to a boil, remove from heat; stir in mushrooms.

In a large bowl, combine spaghetti and half the sauce to coat well. Add turkey and rest of sauce; blend very thoroughly. Spoon mixture into greased baking pans. Sprinkle cheese on top. Bake at 350° F for 45 to 50 minutes until hot through.

Pan sizes	6 pans (9x13x2) or 3 pans (12x18)	10 pans (9x13x2) or 5 pans (12x18)

Cook's Note: Increase baking time to 1 hour if using 12x18x2 pans. If your bowls are not large enough to allow ample mixing room, use two bowls, placing spaghetti in one bowl and turkey in another. Add half the sauce to each bowl, mixing thoroughly. Combine both mixtures before putting in pans.

Sweet and Sour Turkey

	50 SERVINGS	75 SERVINGS
boneless skinless turkey breast	12 pounds	18 pounds
pineapple chunks, drained (reserve juice)	6 cups	9 cups
green pepper, cut in 1/2 inch wide strips	3 cups	4 1/2 cups
Sweet and Sour sauce (recipe below)	10-12 cups	15-17 cups

Cut turkey into finger-size strips; divide among pans. Scatter pineapple chunks and green pepper strips over turkey, dividing evenly among the pans. Pour Sweet and Sour Sauce over the top. Cover tightly with foil; bake at 350º F for 1 hour. Uncover and bake 10 minutes longer. Serve over fluffy rice.

Pan sizes	6 pans (9x13x2) or 3 pans (12x18)	9 pans (9x13x2) or 4 pans (12x18)

Sweet and Sour Sauce

catsup	5 cups	7 1/2 cups
cider vinegar	2 cups	3 cups
brown sugar, packed	1 1/2 cups	2 1/4 cups
pineapple juice	3 cups	4 1/2 cups
cornstarch	2/3 cup	1 cup

Combine all ingredients and cook over medium heat, stirring continuously, until mixture comes to a boil. Lower heat; cook a few minutes longer until sauce thickens and "clears."

Yield (approximately)	10 1/2 cups	15 1/2 cups

Noodles Romanoff

	50 SERVINGS	*75 SERVINGS*
medium noodles, cooked and drained	3 pounds	4 1/2 pounds
margarine	1 1/2 cups	2 1/4 cups
flour	3/4 cup	1 cup + 2 Tablespoons
salt	1 Tablespoon	1 1/2 Tablespoons
onion powder	1 1/2 teaspoons	2 1/4 teaspoons
garlic powder	3/8 teaspoon	1/2 teaspoon
milk	6 cups	9 cups
sour cream	3 cups	4 1/2 cups
small curd cottage cheese	4 1/2 cups	6 3/4 cups
paprika	1 1/2 teaspoons	2 1/4 teaspoons
grated Parmesan cheese	1 1/2 cups	2 1/4 cups
shredded cheese (Monterey Jack or mild cheddar)	3 cups	4 1/2 cups

While noodles are cooking make the sauce. In a large kettle, melt margarine over medium heat. Whisk in flour, salt, onion powder, and garlic powder to blend. Gradually add milk, blending well. Cook over medium heat until mixture comes to a boil, stirring constantly to prevent sticking. Lower heat, cook and stir until thickened (about 5 minutes). Remove from heat and cool slightly. Stir in sour cream, cottage cheese, paprika, and Parmesan cheese; blend very thoroughly. Stir in noodles, tossing gently to completely coat the noodles. Spoon into greased baking pans. Sprinkle with shredded cheese. Bake at 375º F for 1 hour or until hot through and bubbly.

Pan sizes	6 pans (9x13x2) or 2 pans (12x18)	9 pans (9x13x2) or 3 pans (12x18)

Spaghetti and Cheese

	50 SERVINGS	75 SERVINGS
spaghetti, cooked and drained (do not rinse)	3 pounds	4 1/2 pounds
shredded cheese (your choice)	21 cups	30 cups
flour	7 Tablespoons	2/3 cup
dry mustard	3 1/2 teaspoons	5 teaspoons
salt (or to taste)	2 Tablespoons + 1 teaspoon	3 Tablespoons + 1 teaspoon
pepper	7/8 teaspoon	1 1/4 teaspoons
milk	17 1/2 cups (4 1/3 quarts)	25 cups (6 1/4 quarts)
eggs, beaten	14	20
margarine, diced in 1/2 inch pieces	7/8 cup	1 1/4 cups
paprika (to sprinkle on top)		

Divide 1/3 of the spaghetti among the baking pans; sprinkle with 1/3 of the cheese. Repeat twice, making 3 layers. In a small bowl combine flour, dry mustard, salt, and pepper. Stir in enough of the milk to make a smooth paste. In a large bowl beat the eggs; add remaining milk and flour mixture, mixing to blend thoroughly. Pour over spaghetti and cheese (about 3 cups for each 9x13 pan). Dot each 9x13 pan with 2 Tablespoons of diced margarine. Sprinkle lightly with paprika. Bake at 350° F for about 45 minutes or until set in the center. (Test by inserting the blade of a table knife near the center. It should come out clean.) Remove pans from oven and allow to stand 5 to 10 minutes before serving.

Pan sizes	7 pans (9x13x2) or 3 pans (12x18)	10 pans (9x13x2) or 5 pans (12x18)

Cook's Note: The larger size pans will require increased baking time to allow mixture to cook in the center. Cut into squares to serve if desired.

Ranch Potato Casserole

	50 SERVINGS	75 SERVINGS
medium potatoes, peeled	21 pounds	30 pounds
sour cream	3 1/2 cups	5 cups
prepared Ranch dressing	3 1/2 cups	5 cups
parsley flakes	2 1/2 Tablespoons	4 Tablespoons
bacon, cooked, drained and crumbled (optional)	1 3/4 cups	2 1/2 cups
shredded cheese, DIVIDED	10 1/2 cups	15 cups
cornflake crumbs	14 cups	20 cups
melted margarine	1 3/4 cups	2 1/2 cups

Cut potatoes into quarters; cook in boiling salted water until tender. Drain and set aside. Mix together the sour cream, Ranch dressing, parsley flakes, bacon, and 2/3 of the cheese. (Reserve the rest for topping.) Add dressing mixture to the potatoes and mix gently. Turn into greased baking pans. Sprinkle with remaining cheese. Combine the cornflake crumbs and melted margarine; spread over top of cheese. Bake at 350º F for about 45 minutes or until hot through.

Pan sizes	7 pans (9x13x2) or 3 pans (12x18)	10 pans (9x13x2) or 5 pans (12x18)

Picnic Baked Beans

	50 SERVINGS	75 SERVINGS
canned white (navy) beans, drained, LIQUID RESERVED	32 cups	48 cups
onion powder	2 Tablespoons + 2 teaspoons	4 Tablespoons
catsup	4 cups	6 cups
brown sugar, packed	4 cups	6 cups
molasses	6 1/2 Tablespoons	1/2 cup + 2 Tablespoons
dry mustard	2 Tablespoons + 2 teaspoons	4 Tablespoons
reserved liquid from beans	4 cups	6 cups

Mix all ingredients together. Divide into pans. Cover with foil. Bake at 350° F for 2 hours. Remove foil; stir well. Continue baking another 1 to 1 1/2 hours until as thick as desired, stirring every 30 minutes. If needed, add a little more of the reserved bean liquid as beans cook down. 50 SERVINGS makes two 12x18x2 pans; 75 SERVINGS makes three 12x18x2 pans.

Cook's Note: You may add cooked, diced ham or sliced frankfurters to the beans during the last hour of baking if you like.

Yankee Fried Rice

	50 SERVINGS	75 SERVINGS
diced onion	3 cups	4 1/2 cups
margarine	1 1/2 cups	2 1/4 cups
long-grain white rice	9 cups	13 1/2 cups
water	16 1/2 cups	25 cups
chicken bouillon cubes	6	9
salt	3 teaspoons	4 1/2 teaspoons
pepper	3/4 teaspoon	1 1/8 teaspoons

It is best to divide these large quantities between 2 large heavy-bottomed pans. Over medium heat, sauté onion in margarine until transparent. Add the rice and cook, stirring constantly with a wide, flat spatula, until rice is a rich deep golden brown. (This will be darker than for the usual rice pilaf.) Lower heat as needed to prevent burning. Remove from heat and SLOWLY pour in water to prevent a rush of hot steam. Add seasonings and stir; bring to a boil then reduce heat to very low. Cover and simmer about 20 minutes until rice is tender and all liquid is absorbed. Fluff with a fork.

Fruit Cocktail Bars

	60 SERVINGS	80 SERVINGS
eggs	*6*	*8*
sugar	*4 1/2 cups*	*6 cups*
fruit cocktail with juice	*6 cups*	*8 cups*
vanilla	*3 teaspoons*	*4 teaspoons*
flour	*6 3/4 cups*	*9 cups*
baking soda	*4 1/2 teaspoons*	*2 Tablespoons*
salt	*3 teaspoons*	*4 teaspoons*
flaked coconut	*4 cups*	*5 1/3 cups*
chopped walnuts	*1 1/2 cups*	*2 cups*
Glaze (recipe follows)		

Beat together the eggs and sugar; add fruit cocktail with its juice and vanilla and mix well. In a bowl, combine the flour, baking soda, and salt. Stir into fruit mixture and blend well. Spread in greased baking pans. Sprinkle coconut and nuts evenly over the top. Bake at 350° F for 20 to 25 minutes or until a wooden pick inserted in the center comes out clean. Cool 10 minutes before drizzling with glaze. Cool completely before cutting into 2 1/2 x 3 inch pieces.

Glaze

sugar	*1 1/2 cups*	*2 cups*
margarine	*3/4 cup*	*1 cup*
milk	*1/3 cup*	*1/2 cup*
vanilla	*3/4 teaspoon*	*1 teaspoon*

Combine sugar, margarine, and milk in a saucepan. Bring to a boil over low heat. Remove from heat and stir in vanilla. Drizzle over warm bars.

Pan sizes	3 pans (10x15x1)	4 pans (10x15x1)

Glazed Apple-Orange Bars

	60 SERVINGS	80 SERVINGS
light brown sugar, packed	3 cups	4 cups
margarine	1 cup + 2 Tablespoons	1 1/2 cups
applesauce	1 1/2 cups	2 cups
orange peel, shredded	1 Tablespoon	4 teaspoons
eggs	3	4
vanilla	3 teaspoons	4 teaspoons
flour	3 3/4 cups	5 cups
baking powder	3 teaspoons	4 teaspoons
salt	1 1/2 teaspoons	2 teaspoons
baking soda	3/4 teaspoon	1 teaspoon
chopped walnuts	1 1/2 cups	2 cups
Orange Glaze (recipe follows)		

In a saucepan, combine brown sugar and margarine. Cook over low heat, stirring until melted. Remove from heat. Blend in applesauce, orange peel, eggs, and vanilla. In a bowl combine flour, baking powder, salt, and baking soda. Gradually add to applesauce mixture. Add nuts and mix well. Spread into greased baking pans. Bake at 350º F for about 15 minutes or until a wooden pick inserted in the center comes out clean. Cool slightly. Drizzle with glaze. Cool completely before cutting into 2 1/2 x 3 inch bars.

Orange Glaze

powdered sugar, sifted	4 1/2 cups	6 cups
vanilla	1 1/2 teaspoons	2 teaspoons
orange juice	1/3 to 1/2 cup	1/2 to 2/3 cup

Combine all ingredients in a small bowl until smooth. Drizzle over warm bars.

Pan sizes	3 pans (10x15x1)	4 pans (10x15x1)

Apple Crunch

	60 SERVINGS	75 SERVINGS
sugar	1 1/2 cups	1 3/4 cups
cinnamon	2 Tablespoons	2 1/2 Tablespoons
peeled, thinly sliced apples	35 cups	42 cups
flour	6 cups	7 1/2 cups
brown sugar, packed	6 cups	7 1/2 cups
margarine, cut into 1/2 inch pieces	3 cups	3 3/4 cups

Combine sugar and cinnamon. Sprinkle over apple slices and toss to coat evenly. Spread apples in greased 9x13x2 pans. Stir together the flour and brown sugar; add margarine pieces and cut in (or mix with your nice clean fingers) until crumbly. Sprinkle mixture over apples. Bake at 325° F for 1 hour or until topping is golden brown. Serve warm or at room temperature. Serving quantities based on 15 servings per pan.

Pan sizes	4 pans (9x13x2)	5 pans (9x13x2)

Peach Crisp

	60 SERVINGS	75 SERVINGS
canned peach slices, drained	3 large no. 10 cans	4 large no. 10 cans
sugar	1/2 cup	1/2 cup + 2 Tablespoons
cinnamon	2 teaspoons	2 1/2 teaspoons

Topping

oatmeal	8 cups	10 cups
brown sugar, packed	4 cups	5 cups
flour	2 cups	2 1/2 cups
margarine, melted	2 2/3 cups	3 1/3 cups

Divide the drained peaches evenly among the pans. Combine sugar and cinnamon; sprinkle over peaches. In a bowl, combine oatmeal, brown sugar, and flour; stir in melted margarine to blend thoroughly. Sprinkle the crunchy mixture over peaches. Bake at 375° F for about 30 minutes or until topping is golden brown. Serve warm or at room temperature. Serving quantities based on 15 servings per pan.

Pan sizes	4 pans (9x13x2)	5 pans (9x13x2)

Can Size Equivalents

Can Size	Approximate Net Weight	Approximate Cups per Can	Number of Servings
No. 10	6 pounds to 7 pounds 5 oz	12 to 13	25
No. 2 1/2	26 to 30 ozs	3 1/2	5 to 6
No. 2	20 oz	2 1/2	4 to 5
No. 303	1 pound	2	4

Measurement Equivalents

US Measurement	US Equivalent	Metric Equivalent
1 teaspoon	1/3 Tablespoon	5 milliliters
1 Tablespoon	3 teaspoons	15 milliliters
1 ounce (liquid)	2 Tablespoons	
1/4 cup	4 Tablespoons	approx. 60 milliliters
1 cup	16 Tablespoons	.473 liter
1 quart	4 cups	.946 liter
1 gallon	4 quarts	3.785 liters
1 ounce (weight)		approx. 30 grams
1 pound (weight)	16 ounces	.454 kilograms

Metric Measurement	Metric Equivalent	US Equivalent
1 liter (liquid)	1000 milliliters	1.06 quarts
250 milliliters		approx. 1 cup
500 milliliters		approx. 1 pint
1 kilogram (weight)	1000 grams	2.2 pounds
1 gram (weight)		.035 ounces
1 decagram (weight)	10 grams	.35 ounces

The Rest of the Story . . .

At some point during their two-week stay, short-term workers (especially first-timers) are likely to shake their heads in wonder and comment on how well organized the mission is and how efficiently it operates—everything running as smoothly as clockwork. Staff members hearing these remarks have to suppress a chuckle. Even while expressing thanks for the kind words, a flash of instant recall brings to mind more than one instance when things didn't go exactly as planned. Let me share a few from the second semester of conference season two years ago. That one was full of challenges and surprises—unexpected visitors, delayed arrivals, malfunctioning equipment, disrupted schedules. For example:

At the beginning of a conference, students usually arrive on Monday afternoon, sometime prior to 6:00 p.m. dinner time. We expected mid-afternoon arrivals for the Belarussian/Ukrainian conference with only Americans—staff, professors, and short-term workers—at the four tables set in the dining room for lunch. At ten minutes to lunch time Patty Crull (staff) met me in the hallway between dining room and kitchen to say, in her calm way, "Jo, two vans of Belarussians just arrived. We will have seventeen more for lunch." I stopped in mid-stride. Seventeen means three more TABLES. When Patty asked what she could do to help, I suggested, a bit distractedly, that she might pray over the pot of Sloppy Joes on the stove.

The next conference we were well prepared for the Estonian group, even if they did arrive by lunch time. This group comes in a large bus. They are on the road two and a half days and arrival times are unpredictable. There are five border crossings between Estonia and Austria and there can be long delays, sometimes three to five hours at a border. We always pray for easy crossings for them. Well, remember the old saying, "Be careful what you pray for—you are sure to get it"? We awoke Monday morning to find twenty-eight Estonians sleeping on the floors in the staff lounge and hallways. They had arrived at 3:30 a.m.

Just when we thought things were going to settle down a bit, our big commercial dish washer had a nervous breakdown just before dinner one evening. For one memorable day, before a repairman could arrive, dishes were washed by hand. I will spare you the soggy details, but bear in mind that we were cooking, serving, and cleaning up for sixty-nine people that day. After a few weeks the unusual becomes so routine it all seems rather funny. There is never a dull moment. Quiet, occasionally, but never dull.

Spring

Summer

Autumn

Winter

Specialties of the Haus
Order Form

Why not organize a great fundraising project to benefit the people you've read about in this book? You can help train leaders in Eastern Europe as well as introduce others to *Specialties of the Haus*. Just let us know how many cookbooks you need.—Dr. Tony Twist

Dear Tony,

Please send me more information about TCM International and Haus Edelweiss. I want to know more about:

___Student Scholarship Program
___Serving at Haus Edelweiss
___TCM Institute Endowment Funds
___Giving stocks, property, securities, etc.
___Estate Planning
___Please send me regular updates about TCM through TCM'S REPORT. (Send to address given below.)

___Please send _____ copies of *Specialties of the Haus* @ $19.95 plus $3.00
         shipping and handling (per copy) to:

Name _____

Address _____

City _____ State or Province _____ ZIP _____

All Prices are in US Dollars.

Choose method of payment below (check one):	_____ cookbooks at @19.95 each = $ _____ Shipping and handling ($3.00 per book) = $ _____ Total amount = $ _____
___Check ___ Money Order ___ Visa ___ MasterCard ___ American Express ___ Discover Card ___ Other	If paying by credit card, fill out card information below: Card Number _____ Expires ___/___ Name on Card _____ Signature _____

Please make check or money order payable to: TCM International, Inc. Mail completed form and payment to:
         TCM International
         Cookbook
         PO Box 24560
         Indianapolis IN 46224

If paying by credit card, you may fax the completed order form to TCM at 317/290-8607 or order through TCM's web page: http://www.tcmi.org

If you would like more information about TCM and its work in Central and Eastern Europe, contact us at one of the following numbers or addresses:

TCM International
6337 Hollister Drive
PO Box 24560
Indianapolis, Indiana 46224
USA

Phone: (317) 299-0333

FAX: (317) 290-8607

E-mail: tcm@tcmi.org
Web page: www.tcmi.org